REVISITING HIND SWARAJ

By the Same Author

- Mahatma Gandhi on Ethics
- Inspiring Thoughts of Sonia Gandhi
- World Crisis and the Gandhian Way with S. Narayanasamy

About the Author

Dr. Anil Dutta Mishra (*b.* 1965) started his career as an Assistant Professor in the Department of Non-violence and Peace Studies, Jain Vishva Bharati University, Ladnun, Rajasthan. His area of specialization includes Public Administration, Grass-root Politics, Gender Issues, Ecology and Human Rights.

Besides a number of research papers in leading professional journals, he has to his credit 16 books including *Problems and Prospects of Working Women in Urban India* (1994); *Fundamentals of Gandhism* (1995); *Gandhian Approach to Contemporary Problems* (1996); *Decentralized Planning in India : A Study of Objectives and Operational Framework* (1999); *Gender Perspectives : Participation, Empowerment and Development* (1999); *Perspectives on Human Rights* (2002); *Rediscovering Gandhi* (2002); *Patterns of Gender Violence* (2002); *Challenges of Twenty First Century and Gandhian Alternative* (2003); *India and Canada; Past, Present and Future* (2003); *Public Governance and Decentralization : Essays in Honour of T.N. Chaturvedi* (2003); *Gandhian Alternative to Contemporary Problems* (2004); *Globalization Myth and Reality* (2004); *Gandhian Alternative* Vol. III, *Socio-Political Thought* (2005); *Inspiring Thoughts of Mahatma Gandhi* (2008); and *Terrorism : A Global Challenge* (2009) and *Mahatma Gandhi on Ethics* (2010).

REVISITING HIND SWARAJ

Dr. Anil Dutta Mishra

CONCEPT PUBLISHING COMPANY PVT. LTD.
NEW DELHI-110 059

ISBN-13: 978-81-8069-716-6

First Published 2010

Published and Printed by

Concept
Since 1974

Concept Publishing Company Pvt. Ltd.

Regd. Office:

A/15-16, Commercial Block, Mohan Garden
New Delhi-110059 (India)
Phones : 25351460, 25351794, *Fax* : 091-11-25357109
Email : publishing@conceptpub.com
Website: www.conceptpub.com

Editorial Office:

H-13, Bali Nagar, New Delhi-110 015, India.

Cataloging in Publication Data--*Courtesy:* D.K. Agencies (P) Ltd. <docinfo@dkagencies.com>

Gandhi, *Mahatma*, 1869-1948.
[Hinda svarāja. English]
Revisiting Hind swaraj / Anil Dutta Mishra.
p. cm.
Translated from Gujarati.
Includes index.
Contents: pt. 1. Hind swaraj : an introduction -- pt. 2. Hind swaraj or Indian home rule / by M.K. Gandhi.
ISBN 9788180697166

1. Nationalism--India. 2. India--Politics and government--1919-1947. 3. Gandhi, Mahatma, 1869-1948. Hinda svarāja. I. Mishra, Anil Dutta, 1965- II. Title.

DDC 954.035 22

Dedicated to

Dr. Bindeshwar Pathak, a True Gandhian

who has championed sanitation and upliftment of the untouchables as mission of his life and for the last thirty-five years he has been working relentlessly to bring the marginalized sections of the society in the mainstream. He has given voice, dignity and self-respect to the poor scavengers. After Mahatma Gandhi, Dr. Pathak is the only man, who is working to transform the Indian society on Gandhian line. He has given new dimension and meaning to the Gandhian Thought and Action.

Prelude

Hind Swaraj is a unique philosophical text written in dialogue form in 1909. It is a dialogue on the sea. The writer Mohan Das Karamchand Gandhi is himself a Reader and an Editor. In fact Hind Swaraj is the Gandhian bible, it is the sacred book the Father of the Nation gave to country, truly the *Gita* of the nationalist era. The unique beauty of *Hind Swaraj* is that every time you go through it, you will get new interpretation and new insight.

Through *Hind Swaraj* Gandhi wanted to establish self-esteem of individual and moral regeneration of India. In other words, Gandhi through *Hind Swaraj* wanted to transform (a) India as a nation and polity; and (b) Indians. *Hind Swaraj* is a source book for evaluation of India and Indians. It is a manual of action for people.

Hind Swaraj is a critique of excessiveness of materialistic western society. It is a pointer to down side of modern civilization, i.e colonialism, neo-colonialism, violence, alienation etc. It is also a pointer to political democracy because political democracy without social democracy is not a democracy at all.

Criticism on railways, lawyers and doctors must be seen as down side of colonialism and neo-colonialism. We must be very careful about how to study *Hind Swaraj*. Firstly, it may be read keeping local, global and contemporary issues in mind. Secondly, it may be read not only via Marxian or gender perspective rather beyond it. Thirdly, it may be classified as basic/dogmatic/internationalism. *Hind Swaraj* must be read with an open eye. Because in India we live in three generations, i.e. (a) village with no electricity and any infrastructure. They still live in inhuman conditions; (b) city with facilities; and

(c) metropolitan cities with all modern facilities. In October 1939, Gandhi had a discussion with the members of the Executive of Gandhi Seva Sangh. He told the members present on the occasion: "I would ask you to read *Hind Swaraj* with my eyes and see therein the chapter on how to make India nonviolent. You cannot build nonviolence on factory civilization, but it can be built on self-contained villages."

Hind Swaraj provides an alternative how an oppressed class can fight. It provides a way to fight against oppression, injustice, extremism, violence etc. It also provides an alternative to individual, society and state.

One can honestly say that Indians love to talk about *Hind Swaraj* but they have neither understood it properly nor transformed its idea or philosophy on ground. It is a source book for evaluation of India and Indians in the post-independent India. Gandhi's words should not be treated as the last words. It needs research, debate, critical analysis with open mind. We have to rediscover and reinterpret Gandhi's works and deeds in the light of content and context. At the same time we have to unlock Gandhi from the so called Gandhians and Gandhian Institutions.

This work will be useful not only for converting the converters but also the young mind, particularly, the youth, who are in search of icon. T.K. Mahadevan in preface to *Dvija: A Prophet Unheard* rightly wrote: Read *Hind Swaraj* if you love the human family and this earth which is our home. Read it if you wish to do your little bit to halt man's race towards self-extinction.

This work would not have been possible in the present form without the support and help from friends and well-wishers. There are a number of persons behind the scene whose ideas, comments and suggestions have been included in the present book. I shall be failing in my duty if I do not record my appreciation to all of them.

First and foremost, I would like to express my sincere gratitude to Shri T.N. Chaturvedi, former Governor of Karnataka, who gave me an opportunity to speak on *Hind Swaraj* in front of august gathering in Indian Institute of Public

Administration. That day I conceived this idea and the result is in front of us in a book form. I have no words to express my heartfelt regards to him.

Within Gandhian circle, I owe my hearty appreciation, affection and loving gratefulness to each and every member particularly, Shri B.H. Jain, Chairman, Jain Irrigation Systems Ltd., Jalgaon, who encouraged me to work on Gandhi.

I am equally grateful to Prof. R.P. Misra, former Vice Chancellor, University of Allahabad, Allahabad; Prof. D. Gopal of IGNOU; Prof. Bidyut Chakrabarty of Delhi University; Prof. J.N. Sharma of Panjab University, Chandigarh; Prof. K.S. Bharati of Nagpur University, Nagpur; Prof. R.P. Dwivedi of Kashi Vidyapeeth, Varanasi; Prof. Amita Singh of JNU; Dr. A.K. Dubey, IAS; Mr. Atul Tiwari, IAS; Mr. Prabhat Ranjan, IRTS; Dr. Pravin Kumar of Delhi University; Prof. M.P. Dubey of Allahabad University; Dr. Rajshekhar Basu of Calcutta University; Dr. Anurag Gungal of Jammu University; Dr. H.S. Rathore of Jodhpur University; Dr. Devendra Kakar and Dr. Anju Jhamb of Delhi University, for guidance and cooperation.

As always, I received full support and patience of my dear family when I was busy with completion of this volume. My special thanks are due to my wife Dr. Sweta Mishra, Assistant Professor, Gargi College , University of Delhi, Delhi, and my daughters, Sanstuti and Sansriti for their patience and help.

My special thanks to my brother Sunil Dutta Mishra, ADJ, and Purushottam Tripathi, Advocate for helping and encouraging me to complete the work on time.

Last but not the least, I am grateful to Shri Ashok Kumar Mittal, Concept Publishing Company Pvt. Ltd., for bringing out the book in a nice form and that too within record time.

Salkhani, Bihar **Anil Dutta Mishra**
15th November, 2009

Contents

PART ONE

HIND SWARAJ : AN INTRODUCTION

1

Hind Swaraj : An Introduction

Hind Swaraj is Mahatma Gandhi's unique and fundamental work. It is an Indian contribution to Political Theory after Kautilya's *Arthashastra*. Gandhi was a political activist responding creatively to the socio-political and economic circumstances in which he was located. *Hind Swaraj* is an alternative to modern socio-economic-political thought. It is a book, which cannot be ignored in any discussion and debate on human progress, socio-economic development and contemporary problems. It is a key to understanding not only Gandhi's life and thought but also the present dilemmas arising out of technology, industrialization and globalization. *Hind Swaraj* still continues to evoke critical interest the world over even now. It is not only a book on how to win political freedom for India. It is a *magna carta* for the freedom of mind and the evolution of human species from conscious and material beings to superconscious and moral beings.[1] In fact *Hind Swaraj* is a manifesto for a new world order based on supremacy of ethics and morality over matter. It still represents voice of the voiceless, voice of the common man of India, and even of the common people of the whole world.

Hind Swaraj is one of the earliest of those few books which Gandhi wrote during his hectic public life. All other writings of Gandhi are in the form of articles, statements, letters and speeches. *Hind Swaraj* has a pivotal position in his writings, because in this small but 'severe' booklet is contained Gandhi's ideas, and which Mahadev Desai has aptly termed "seminal".

1. R.P. Misra, *Hind Swaraj*, New Delhi, Concept Publishing Company, 2006 (Under Publication).

The book, to quote Gandhi's own words has had a "chequered career".[1]

Margaret Chaterjee called *Hind Swaraj* 'a very basic document for the study of Gandhi's thought'. B.R. Nanda called it Gandhi's 'confession of faith'. Erik Erikson called it 'a rather incendiary manifesto'. Dennis Dalton called it 'a proclamation of ideological independence.' And Judith Brown called it 'the nearest he came to producing a sustained work of political theory'. Similarly, Gerald Heard compared *Hind Swaraj* with Rousseau's *Social Contract*. George Catlin (1950) compared it with *The Spiritual Exercises* of St. Ignatitus Loyala.[2]

Hind Swaraj is a work, which Gandhi himself translated from Gujarati into English. *Hind Swaraj* is the seed from which the tree of Gandhian thought has grown to its full stature. For those interested in Gandhian thought in a general way, it is the right place to start; for it is here that he presents his basic ideas in their proper relationship to one another. And for those who wish to study his thought more methodically, it remains the norm by which to assess the theoretical significance of his other writings including the Autobiography.[3]

The unique beauty of the *Hind Swaraj* lies in its capacity to present a very scientific and philosophical discourse in the most ordinary language. In other words the book is written in perfectly Gandhian style-terse, simple and logical. The basic feature of *Hind Swaraj* is that every time you go through it, you will get a new interpretation and a new insight. It is in *Hind Swaraj* that we find Gandhi first announcing his own life-mission. This is nothing other than showing the way for the moral regeneration of Indians and the political emancipation of Mother India. *Hind Swaraj* teaches "*the gospel of love in place of that of hate. It replaces violence with self-sacrifice. It pits soul force against brute force*".[4]

1. Nageshwar Prasad (Ed.), *Hind Swaraj: A Fresh Look*, New Delhi, Gandhi Peace Foundation, 1985, p. 1.
2. Anthony J. Parel, *Hind Swaraj and Other Writings*, Cambridge, Cambridge University Press, 1997, p. XII.
3. *Ibid.*, p. XIII.
4. Mahatma Gandhi, *Hind Swaraj or Indian Home Rule*, Ahmedabad, Navajivan Publishing House, 1938, p. 13.

Context of Hind Swaraj

The immediate context of writing the booklet was Gandhi's encounter with the Indian anarchists in England and their cult of violence. It is not only the cult of violence that provoked Gandhi to write this tract. On the contrary, it goes much deeper and is more comprehensive in its sweep. The entire Western or material civilization forms the very backbone of his critique.[1]

One can discover three issues clearly emerging in *Hind Swaraj.* First is the then current politics in India, its leaders and political events and Gandhi's own position in relation to them. Second, and rather the most crucial issue is the entire question of material or 'modern' civilization. And, lastly, there is the question of passive resistance that is posited as an alternative to what Gandhi calls the brute force.[2]

In *Hind Swaraj,* three streams of thought merge and what emerges is a manifesto warning against what Gandhi called the mad race after civilization or (according to more recent usage) modernization. *Hind Swaraj* is a critique of modernization, which in Gandhi's words is identified with the Western, material, modern civilization. The critique does not stop there. One can discover the contours of what he called, "the whole theory of life," emerging from the discussion recorded therein. It is a theory of life, which is not static. No theory, which seeks to build up an alternative to the one in vogue, can be static. It is, indeed, a dynamic model theory, which acquires greater precision as Gandhi's experiences through his public life accumulate. Mahatma Gandhi considers 'Parliament' and 'machinery' to be the mainstay of modern civilization and, therefore, warns against their importation.[3]

On October 9, 1909, Gandhi[4] wrote to Lord Ampthill a letter, which contains ideas, which formed the bases of *Hind Swaraj :*

1. Nageshwar Prasad, p. 16.
2. *Ibid.*
3. *Ibid.*, pp. 16-17.
4. D.G. Tendulkar, *Mahatma,* Vol. 1, Bombay, Vithalbhai K. Jhaveri, 1951, pp. 127-28.

1. Impatience with the British rule was widespread in India and so was the hatred of the British;
2. The above being the case, repression would be counter-productive;
3. British people were obsessed with commercial selfishness and hence the British Government would not concede the rights of the Indians;
4. The fault lies not with the British people but with modern civilization which is a negation of the spirit of Christianity;
5. All that shines as modern—the railways, machines, the style of life etc., are a true badge of slavery of the Indian people, as they are of Europeans;
6. Rise of large cities like Calcutta and Bombay was a matter of sorrow, not of congratulation;
7. India has lost because her villages are destroyed;
8. Violent methods are built in the modern civilization and so is immorality;
9. I share the national spirit but I do not agree with those who want to use violence directly or indirectly to win freedom for the country because it is immoral and against the spirit of Indian civilization;
10. Rulers must rule according to the wishes of the people; the moment they fail in their primary duty, people must refuse to recognize them and cooperate with them.

Hind Swaraj raises fundamental questions. India's encounter with Britain was not political and economic but civilizational. Even today, the situation is no different from the one when Gandhi wrote *Hind Swaraj*. For proper understanding of *Hind Swaraj*, it is necessary to refer to the historical context of *Hind Swaraj*, which, in the main, consisted of six situations or developments :

(a) the general developments in India since 1857;
(b) the emergence of new professional classes;
(c) the circumstances prevailing in India with special reference to the partition of Bengal;

(d) the Russia-Japanese War, and the revolutionary fervour in Czarist Russia;
(e) the situation in South Africa and Gandhi's experiences and experiments there; and
(f) the immediate provocation for Gandhi to write *Hind Swaraj*.[1]

The book is addressed to a mixed audience: the expatriate Indians greatly attracted to terrorism and political violence, the Extremists and Moderates of the Indian National Congress, the Indian nation (means ordinary Indians), and the English (means both the British ruling class living in India and Britons living in Great Britain).

As to why Gandhi wrote the book, there was first of all the question of an inner illumination and the consequent urge to communicate. Gandhi's intentions in writing *Hind Swaraj* have been grouped by Anthony J. Parel[2] under six rubrics. These are:

(1) Gandhi harboured the ideas contained in *Hind Swaraj* for quite some time. Gandhi was inpatient to communicate them to people around him and world over specially the Indians who were his immediate concern,
(2) He wanted to clarify the meaning of *Swaraj*, which was far wider and deeper than political independence,
(3) Gandhi wanted to reopen a peaceful path of conflict resolution perfected by Indian civilisation and convince the people of India, especially the youth, to abjure terrorism and return to the Indian way,
(4) Gandhi wanted to tell his countrymen that it was not the British colonialism, which was their real enemy. The real enemy was Western Civilisation. So long as they remain mesmerized by Western Civilisation, they

1. Devdutt, *Hind Swaraj: Context and Text*, in Nageshwar Prasad (Ed.), *Hind Swaraj: A Fresh Look*, New Delhi, Gandhi Peace Foundation, 1985, p. 30.
2. R.P. Misra, *op. cit.*

would remain salves even if they get political independence,

(5) Gandhi was keen to see that Indians and British part political company as friends, not as enemies. He did not consider the British to be the enemies of Indians; the enemy was the modern (industrial) civilisation, which afflicted them both, and

(6) He wanted to use *Hind Swaraj* as a vehicle to give to India an updated version of *dharma*, which even a common man could understand and which would fit its people for life in the modern world. "I have used the language of politics, but I have really tried to offer a glimpse of *dharma*". Thus Gandhi wanted to make British occupation of India as an opportunity to realise fully the potential of Indian civilisation.

Parel[1] then looks into the historical contexts in which Gandhi wrote the *Hind Swaraj*. These contexts include :

(1) The hold of modern industrial civilisation on the minds of the people all over the world, especially in the West. *Hind Swaraj* challenged this civilisation and branded it as satanic. According to Parel, "Its critique of that civilisation is one of its main contributions to modern political thought".While criticizing modern civilisation, Gandhi was not negative and vindictive. He commended some of its contributions which Indian civilisation lacked or did not pay the attention they deserved—civil liberty, equality, human rights, prospects of improving the economic conditions of the poors, emancipation of women from tradition and religious toleration. He was critical because its tendencies were lopsided, because its concept and practice of freedom did not amount to *Swaraj*, in fact it negated it. It promoted rights at the cost of duties, economic progress at the cost of moral and spiritual

1. *Ibid.*

progress, and divided the world into We and They using religion, political dispensation, economic status, military might, education, etc. as dividers. It negated human brotherhood and the concept of *vasudhaiva kutumbakam*.

(2) The political situation in South Africa where he evolved as a Mahatma was another historical context in which *Hind Swaraj* was written. It was in South Africa that he first acquired the vision of Indian nationalism. In fact South Africa was the foundation on which he realised himself as a leader. Parel rightly says that South Africa enabled him to transcend colonialism as the cause of the plight of Indians there. The culprit was the modern civilisation, which had caught the whole humanity by its neck.
South Africa freed Gandhi from man of the constraints he would have got, had he been in India. He could not work without any social and religious pressures but also experiment with his ideas in places like Phoenix settlement. But for his being in South Africa, he would not have got the opportunity to go to London on lobbying missions in 1906 and 1909 and thus acquire his diplomatic skills.

(3) The third historical context Parel identifies is the politics of expatriate Indians, especially of those based in London, which centred on preparation for violent struggle against the British. This brought Gandhi closer to many of the revolutionaries and prompted him to write *Hind Swaraj*.

(4) The Indian nationalist movement was yet another context in which the book was written by Gandhi.

(5) Gandhi's acquaintance with Western people, philosophers and thoughts was a major factor that shaped and sharpened Gandhi's views contained in *Hind Swaraj*.

The above mentioned ideas were developed in *Hind Swaraj* or Indian Home Rule, a small book of about 30,000 words (96 pages), written in Gujarati on board the ship S.S. Kildonan Castle during Gandhi's return trip from England to South Africa after an abortive mission to London. It was written in ten days between 13 to 22 November, 1909. The whole manuscript was written on the ship's stationery, and the writing went on at such a furious pace that when the right hand got tired Gandhi continued with the left. He worked day and night on the manuscript. Forty of the 275 manuscript pages were written with left hand. And he wrote as if under inspiration. In the entire autograph, only sixteen lines have been scratched out and only a few words changed here and there.[1] As stated by Gandhiji himself: *"I wrote the entire* Hind Swaraj *for my dear friend Dr. Pranjivan Mehta. All the argument in the book is reproduced almost as it took place with him."*[2]

The book first appeared serially in the *Indian Opinion* and later it was published in book form, to be proscribed in March 1910, by the Bombay Government, because it contained *'matter declared to be seditious'*.[3] On that, Gandhi published the English translation from Natal to show the innocuous nature of its contents. The ban was finally lifted on 21 December, 1938. When Gokhale saw the translation, he thought it so crude and hastily conceived that he prophesied that Gandhi himself would destroy the book after spending a year in India. In 1921, Gandhi said: "with deference to the memory of the great teacher, I may say that his prediction has failed to come true." Gandhi writing of the book said: *"I withdraw nothing except one word of it, and that in deference to a lady friend"*.[4]

The *Hind Swaraj* or Indian Home Rule is a severe condemnation of modern civilization. It is divided into twenty chapters and two appendices. It deals in detail with *swaraj*, civilization, lawyers, doctors, machinery, education, passive resistance and other matters. It deals with practical questions in a most scientific and original way. It is written in dialogue form, reaching great heights in some places. It is a faithful

1. Anthony J. Parel, *op. cit.*, p. XIV.
2. CWMG, Vol. 71, p. 238.
3. CWMG, Vol. 10, p. 245.
4. CWMG-CD, Vol. 22, p. 260.

record of conversations he had with workers, one of whom was an avowed terrorist.

Divided into four themes elaborated or enunciated in various parts of the book, viz., (a) core concepts : nonviolence, education, and technology; (b) criticism of Parliament, of machinery and of the Congress view of *swaraj*; (c) *Hind Swaraj* as an assessment and a critique of the Western civilization with reference to non-Western civilization with non-Western criteria; and (d) perception.[1] *Hind Swaraj* is the quintessence of all that Mahatma Gandhi had read, thought and experienced by the age of forty. While a student in England, he came in contact with radical and liberal groups and individuals. It was there that he read extensively, thought deeply and gained first-hand experience of the working of Western civilization. The most distinctive influence on the formation of his ideas was through the works of Tolstoy, Ruskin, Thoreau and Edward Carpenter, all vehement critics of industrial life and advocates of simplicity.

The substance of Gandhi's attacks in *Hind Swaraj* is 'machinery', that is, technology. "It is the chief symbol of modern civilization; it represents a great sin".[2] In *Hind Swaraj* Gandhi declared "Parliament" as a "prostitute and a sterile woman". Indicates that *Hind Swaraj* posits an ideal state of things in which there will be no machine, no railways, no doctors, lawyers and such other things as are the symbols of modern civilization. It is not Rousseau's state of nature, but the ideal society of Marx in which the state will wither away, minus the modern type of technology (machinery) to which the former (Marx) was wedded unconditionally.[3]

Gandhi's thinking about the whole question of industrialization seems to be running along two parallel levels. At one level, Gandhi seems to be concerned with the problem of poverty and unemployment. Gandhi was very clear about this in mind. He knew that the Western pattern of industrialization involved per capita investment of a

1. Devdutt, *op. cit.*, p. 33.
2. M.K. Gandhi, *op. cit.*, p. 94.
3. Nageshwar Prasad, *op. cit.*, p. 17.

magnitude, which India could hardly afford to generate unless it took to authoritarian or totalitarian methods. Gandhi's aim was to revive cottage and village industries. In other words what he was seeking was the resuscitation of the village through the revival of its handicrafts. Must not be supposed that Gandhi believed in the static, archaic mode of production in the village prevalent in the past. He welcomed every improvement in the village craft (small unit) if it led to increase in productivity. The only condition attached was that the improvement must not render people unemployed. He was even willing to accept the use of energy (electricity, etc.) if it could be useful for village industries, in case the village owned the power plant. At another level Gandhi had a more fundamental objection to Western pattern of industrialization. It is in this respect that his approach differs both from the liberal and the Marxian approach. Liberal and the Marxian approaches put their faith in an ever-growing material standard of life. And for this purpose, they depend upon an intensive exploitation of natural resources, minerals and fossil fuels. This leads them to multiply machinery which Gandhi called the 'craze for machinery'. Agriculture, therefore, becomes the backbone for pushing ahead with such a pattern of industrial development. Exploitation of agriculture leads to the growing desolation and ruination of the village and the pauperization of the village population, which eventually finds its sanctuary in the cities, in the slums and in overcrowded, cramped spaces. This leads to an unrestrained urbanization with all its attendant evils of crime, prostitution and has been aptly termed as 'street corner societies'.[1]

A very critical element in Gandhi's critique of modern machine technology is that it leads to conflict among nations and ultimately to war. "Blueprint for Survival," statements by thirty-three of Britain's most distinguished scientists have reaffirmed the faith in Gandhi. Recent critics who question the very basis of its dependence on the present day technology reinforce Gandhi's objection to modern civilization. Since technology is predicated upon increasing consumption of

1. *Ibid.*, pp. 18-19.

natural resources, which, the critics point out, are limited, the entire superstructure of the so-called civilization is threatened with destruction. Gandhi cried a halt to this mad pursuit after indiscriminate multiplication of machinery.[1]

Gandhi questioned all these assumptions. He was not against science as such. Modern science is grounded on two fundamentals. The first is the kind of science which penetrates the nature of reality, tries to go deep into problems of the universe, raises issues of a philosophical nature and tries to establish or reject them by its experiments, and makes an effort through its findings at unification of man with the deeper reality in which he has his being and becoming. But there is yet another dimension of science, that is, the dimension of its application to solving the physical needs of the humankind.[2]

Gandhi warned and suggested restraint. It is in this context that he prescribed the application of science only when its usefulness had been assessed in all its multi-dimensional relationship with man, society and nature. We are witnessing today a civilization crisis. It is a crisis because the entire system of machine technology is in crisis, rather threatened with a crash as sensitive minds, scientists and others, are warning us today. Gandhi was perhaps the first in the present century who realized the deeper and long range implications of this technological progress. His whole response to it is one of caution, restraint and limitation. It originated in *Hind Swaraj* as a response of a particular civilization, namely, of the Indian civilization to the Western. Gandhi's thinking evolved within the orbit of the world developments (including the two World Wars), his response acquired a universal character embracing the whole mankind verging on a precipice where the large scale high technology has brought it.[3]

Gandhi could easily reconcile it with his basic philosophical position. What emerged from this was a way out of the present civilizational crisis. We may now chart out the basic ingredients of the Gandhian scheme. In Gandhi, man

1. *Ibid.*, pp. 20-23.
2. *Ibid.*, p. 23.
3. *Ibid*, pp. 23-24.

emerges at the centre of all social, economic and political development. This man is the spiritual man, aligned and wholly integrated with his community and his surroundings.[1]

Hind Swaraj is a warning against indiscriminate large-scale mechanization of life and a pointer to the future. The rudimentary model presented therein is, as we have indicated, not static. It is, on the contrary, dynamic in so far as it assumes a more sharply defined shape as Gandhi's thinking becomes global in character through time. *Hind Swaraj,* therefore, must be placed within the framework of Gandhi's thought as it developed through his active life.[2]

In *Hind Swaraj,* Gandhi re-opens the debate, which had raged in India in the second half of nineteenth century, and he raised his voice against modern and Western civilization. He also offered a concept of normal society having its roots in India's past and its values. Gandhi revalidated the essence of Indian civilization; he made the plea that it be accepted as the starting point of the next phase of India's growth in order to transform it in the long run. Two other factors determined the format and the content of *Hind Swaraj.* The patriotic Indians in London had come to the conclusion that India should "adopt modern methods of violence and modern civilization to drive out the British."[3]

Gandhi had evolved a different approach to life on the basis of his experiments in South Africa; he disagreed with the patriotic Indians about their diagnosis and prescription.[4] As a point of clarification, we should like to point out that Gandhi's denunciation of railways, lawyers, doctors and parliaments, machinery and brute force should not be taken literally. These have only an emblematic or metaphorical significance. Gandhi means more than what he says.[5] Gandhi enunciates a 19-point programme of action entitled *Chhutkara,* which means "the emancipation".[6]

---

1. *Ibid.*, p. 24.
2. *Ibid.*, p. 28.
3. Devdutt, *op. cit.*, p. 32.
4. *Ibid.*
5. *Ibid.*, p. 35.
6. *Ibid.*, p. 38.

Hind Swaraj provides a scathing critique of Western civilization. The three recurrent themes are (i) colonial imperialism; (ii) industrial capitalism; and (iii) rationalist materialism.[1] According to Gandhi, colonialism triumphed in India not because of its strength but because of Indians' inherent weaknesses, which allowed 'this intimate enemy' to take root. Gandhi was the first person to have attributed the British rule in India to a 'moral decline' affecting the entire nation.[2] Attributing colonialism in India to 'our weakness', Gandhi thus argued that '*The English have not taken India; we have given it to them. They are not in India because of their strength, but because we keep them....*'.[3] According to Gandhi, the British conquest of India was solely due to the Indians' moral failure.[4] In *Hind Swaraj* Gandhi produced the most effective trans-cultural protest against the hyper-masculine worldview of colonialism. In other words, *Hind Swaraj* is the most creative response to the perversion of industrial capitalism.[5] For Gandhi, industrialization remained the driving force behind Western civilization. 'Machinery is the chief symbol of modern civilization; it represents a great sin...If the machine craze grows in our country, it will become an unhappy land.'[6] 'It is necessary to realize that machinery is bad. We shall then be able gradually to do away with it ... If, instead of welcoming machinery as a boon, we should look it as an evil, it would ultimately go.'[7] According to Gandhi, 'a snake-bite is a lesser poison than the mill industry because, while the former merely harmed the body, the latter destroys body, mind and soul.'[8] According to Gandhi, there remained a tension between true civilization and a civilization based on machine. While the former is based on brute rationalist materialism, the latter

1. Bidyut Chakrabarty, *Social and Political Thought of Mahatma Gandhi*, London, Routledge, 2006, p. 24.
2. *Ibid.*
3. M.K. Gandhi, *op. cit.*, p. 24.
4. Bidyut Chakrabarty, *op. cit.* p. 25.
5. *Ibid.*
6. M.K. Gandhi, *op. cit.*, p. 81.
7. *Ibid.*, pp. 83-84.
8. *Ibid.*, p. 82.

draws its sustenance from *dharma*. In modern civilization, *artha* (money) and *kama* (desire) are totally divorced from *dharma* on the basis of the alleged superiority of rational materialism.[1]

On the one hand, *Hind Swaraj* was Gandhi's creative response to the theoretical basis of Western civilization. Drawing on the civilizational resources of Hindu religion and its tradition, he put forward a new theoretical framework to conceptualize both colonialism and industrial capitalism. On the other hand he developed the fundamental precepts of what later became Gandhism. The three important themes that recur not only in his writings but also in his deeds are *swaraj, swadeshi* and *satya*. *Swaraj* was rule of self by the self. It was therefore more than a political idea to the Mahatma it meant India's spiritual liberation through a fundamental change in each individual's perception. *Swadeshi,* which meant self-respect, self-realization and self-reliance was not merely glorification of traditional and indigenous methods of production but a creative application of the available means meaningful to the people in consideration. His debate is not on *'whether India needs technology'*; his debate is on *'the kind of technology that India needs'*. *Satya* is truth-force and only *ahimsa*. Together with *ahimsa, satya* constituted *satyagraha*. It was a method of securing rights by personal suffering. *Satyagraha* was an indigenous combination of reason, morality and politics; it appealed to the opponent's head, heart and interests.[2]

Contents of Hind Swaraj

The opening chapters 1-3 deal with the Indian National Congress and the Indian awakening. Chapter 4 explains the true meaning of Swaraj. A critique of modern industrial civilization is presented in chapters 5 and 6. The pitiable condition of India is elaborated in chapters 7 to 12. Why Gandhi considered the Indian civilization to be a truly modern

1. Bidyut Chakrabarty, *op. cit.*, p. 26.
2. *Ibid.*, pp. 26-27.

civilization is given in chapter 13. The potency of *satyagraha* or passive resistance is explained in chapters 14 to 17. Chapters 18 and 19 discuss the problem associated with modern education and technology. The last chapter 20 gives conclusions. Appendix I lists twenty references for further reading, including six by Tolstoy, two by Thoreau, two by Ruskin, one by Plato (Defence and Death of Socrates), and one by Mazzini (Duties of Man), and one each by Dadabhai Naoroji, and R.C. Dutt on the economic condition of colonial India. Appendix II lists Testimonies by Eminent men.

In a letter to a friend in India, Gandhi[1] summarized the contents of *Hind Swaraj* in the following words:

1. There is no impassable barrier between East and West.
2. There is no such thing as western or European civilization, but there is a modern civilization which is purely material.
3. The people of Europe, before they were touched by modern civilization, had much in common with the people of the East; anyhow the people of India, and even today Europeans who are not touched by modern civilization, are far better able to mix with Indians than the offspring of that civilization.
4. It is not the British people who are ruling India, but it is modern civilization, through its railways, telegraph, telephone, and almost every invention, which has been claimed to be a triumph of civilization.
5. Bombay, Calcutta, and other chief cities of India are the real plague-spots.
6. If British rule were replaced tomorrow by Indian rule based on modern methods, India would be no better, except that she would be able to retain some of the money that is drained away to England; but then India would only become a second or fifth nation of Europe or America.
7. East and West can really meet when the West has thrown overboard the modern civilization, almost in

1. D.G. Tendulkar, *op.cit.*, pp. 129-31.

its entirety. They can also seemingly meet when East has also adopted modern civilization, but that meeting would be an armed truce, even as it is between, say, Germany and England, both of which nations are living in the Hall of Death in order to avoid being devoured, the one by the other.

8. It is simply impertinence for any man or anybody of men to being or contemplate reform of the whole world. To attempt to do so by means of highly artificial and speedy locomotion is to attempt the impossible.
9. Increase of material comforts, it may be generally laid down, does not in any way whatsoever conduce to moral growth.
10. Medical science is the concentrated essence of black magic. Quackery is infinitely preferable to what passes for high medical skill as such.
11. Hospitals are the instruments that the Devil has been using for his own purpose, in order to keep his hold on his kingdom. They perpetuate vice, misery and degradation and real slavery. I was entirely off the track when I considered that I should receive a medical training. It would be sinful for me in any way whatsoever to take part in the abominations that go in the hospitals. If there were no hospitals for venereal diseases, or even for consumptives, we should have less consumption, and less sexual vice against us.
12. India's salvation consists in unlearning what she has learnt during the past fifty years or so. The railways, telegraphs, hospitals, lawyers, doctors, and such like have all to go, and the socalled upper classes have to learn to live consciously and religiously and deliberately the simple life of a peasant knowing it to be a life giving true happiness.
13. India should wear no machine-made clothing whether it comes out of European mills or Indian mills.
14. England can help India to do this and then she will have justified her hold on India. There seems to be many England today who think likewise.

15. There was true wisdom in the ages of old having so regulated society as to limit the material conditions of the people: the rude plough of perhaps five thousand years ago is the plough of the husbandman today. Therein lies salvation. People live long under such conditions, in comparative peace much greater than Europe has enjoyed after having taken up modern activity, and I feel that every enlightened man, certainly every Englishman, may, if he chooses, learn this truth and act according to it.

Similarly R.P. Misra[1] beautifully in a nutshell, summarizes the contents of *Hind Swaraj* :

1. The so called modern civilization is not western civilization because there was no difference between East and West before the modern industrial civilization engulfed the West;
2. The exploitation of the East by the West is not because of the civilization they have been bitten by;
3. India has not been invaded by the British; Indians were so lured by the industrial civilization that they invited the British to rule over them;
4. Exploitative urbanization symbolizes modern civilization;
5. The problem is not the removal of the British and their replacement by Indians but how to change the system to bring in a truly modern civilization;
6. Improvement in the material welfare does not, in any way, uplift man morally. Improvement in the moral standards of life, ennobles even materials progress;
7. Medicine, as it is practiced, is the major cause of diseases;
8. Legal system generates discord among the people; it rarely brings people together;

1. R.P. Misra. *op. cit.*

9. Craze for machinery is a dangerous proposition; labour saving machinery is good if everyone has work for livelihood and creativity;
10. Violence breeds violence; *Satyagraha* is the weapon of strong, not of the weak;
11. Ends and means are inseparable; we cannot achieve noble ends by wrong means. Right means will always lead to right ends;
12. 'Simple living and high thinking' alone can bring peace and harmony;
13. Primary education means moral education;
14. There was true wisdom in the saying of the sages having so regulated society as to limit the material conditions of the people;
15. India will be free the moment Indians cast away the lure of modern civilization.

Gandhi on Hind Swaraj

Writing the introduction to the Gujarati edition, translated and published in the *Indian Opinion* of 22 November, 1909, Gandhi said: *"The views I venture to place before the reader are, needless to say, held by many Indians not touched by what is known as civilization but I ask the reader to believe me when I tell him that they are also held by thousands of Europeans."*[1] However, when the English translation was published, Gandhi wrote a comparatively longer introduction on 20 March, 1910: *"the British Government in India constitutes a struggle between the Modern civilization, which is the Kingdom of Satan, and ancient civilization, which is the Kingdom of God."* In the same year he wrote to Gokhale that the ideas contained in the book *"have been matured in the course of the struggle..."* Again writing to Maganlal Gandhi, he said : *"My present state of mind is such that even if the whole world is against what I have written, I would not be depressed."*[2]

---

1. *CWMG*, Vol. 10, p. 7.
2. *CWMG*, Vol. 10., p. 139.

Gandhi published Mr. Wybergh's criticism written in the form of a letter dated 3 May 1910 in the *Indian Opinion* of 21 May 1910.[1] In reply Gandhi, in his letter dated 10 May 1910 concentrated mainly on an exposition of passive resistance, because most of the remarks in Mr. Wybergh's letter centred round it. However, in answer to Wybergh's criticism of his views on modern civilization, Gandhi categorically stated: *"I have ventured utterly to condemn modern civilization because I hold that the spirit of it is evil. It is possible to show that some of its incidents are good but I have examined its tendency in the scale of ethics."*[2] In 1914, when the second Gujarati edition was brought out, Gandhi wrote: *"I find that the convictions I started in the book have grown stronger."*[3] Further, *"The key to an understanding of* Hind Swaraj *lies in the worldly pursuits should give way to ethical living."*[4] Writing to Maganlal Gandhi in 1919, Gandhi said: *"Besides, the more experience I gain, the more I realize that machinery will keep us in personal slavery and I find what I said it in* Hind Swaraj *is literally true"*.[5] In 1920, answering the critics, he said : *"I do not ask India to follow today the methods prescribed in my booklet. If they could that, they would have* Swaraj *not in a year but in a day. What I am doing today is that I am giving the country a pardonable programme for the attainment of parliamentary Swaraj"*.[6]

In 1921, he carried the explanation still further. In his foreword to the book, he sounded a note of caution to the reader.

"But I must warn the reader against thinking that I am today aiming at the Swaraj *described therein. I know that India is not ripe for it. It may seem an impertinence to say so. But such is the conviction. I am individually working for the self-rule pictured therein. But today my corporate activity is undoubtedly devoted to the attainment of parliamentary* Swaraj *in accordance with the wishes*

1. *CWMG*, Vol. 10., pp. 507-11.
2. *CWMG*, Vol. 10, p. 247.
3. *CWMG*, Vol. 12, p. 411.
4. *CWMG*, Vol. 12, p. 412.
5. *CWMG*, Vol. 15, p. 340.
6. D.G. Tendulkar, *op. cit.*, p. 17.

of the people of India. I am not aiming at destroying railways or hospitals, though I would certainly welcome their natural destruction. Neither railways nor hospitals are a test of a high and pure civilization. At best they are a necessary evil. Neither adds one inch to the moral stature of a nation. Nor am I aiming at a permanent destruction of law courts, much as I regard it as a 'consummation devoutly to be mills. It requires a higher simplicity and renunciation than the people are today prepared for."[1]

In 1924 answering some objections, Gandhi wrote :

"I have nothing to withdraw from what I have written in the Indian Home Rule... *It must be remembered that it is not the Indian Home Rule depicted in that book that I am placing before India. I am placing before the nation parliamentary, i.e., democratic* Swaraj. *I do not suggest today a destruction of all machines, but I am making the spinning-wheel the master machine. The Indian Home Rule depicts an ideal state....The fact that I cannot come up to the ideal condition of things laid down therein is to be attributed to my weakness. What I have said about hospitals is also true. And yet I suppose I shall resort to the few medicines I hold lawful so long as I retain the least attachment for my body."*[2]

In 1929, he wrote to Satis Chandra Dasgupta that *"there is not one word in* Hind Swaraj *that cannot be substantiated if I have to rewrite it today, I may change the language but never the thought."*[3] In 1938, the *Aryan Path* brought out its special number devoted to *Hind Swaraj*. Giving a message to the *Aryan Path* on the eve of the publication of its special number, Gandhi categorically stated :

"I may change the language here and there, if I had to rewrite the booklet. But after the stormy thirty years through which I have passed, I have seen nothing to alter the views expounded therein."[4]

In 1939, a friend, according to Gandhi, pointed out the contradiction between what he wrote in *Hind Swaraj* and what he practiced. Gandhi commented with his usual forthrightness.

1. *CWMG*, Vol. 19, pp. 277-78.
2. *CWMG*, Vol. 24, p. 548.
3. *CWMG*, Vol. 42, p. 125.
4. *CWMG*, Vol. 67, pp. 169-70.

"The Key to understand that incredibly simple (so simple as to be regarded foolish) booklet is to realize that it is not an attempt to go back to the so-called ignorant dark ages. But it is an attempt to see beauty in voluntary simplicity, poverty and slowness. I have pictured that as my ideal. I shall never reach it myself and hence cannot expect the nation to do so. But the modern age is for variety, for flying through the air, for multiplicity of wants, etc. which have no fascination for me. They deaden the inner being in us. The giddy heights which man's ingenuity is attempting, take us away from our Maker who is nearer to us than the nails are to the flesh which they cover."[1]

In October 1939, Gandhi had a discussion with the members of the Executive of Gandhi Seva Sangh. He told the members present on that occasion: *"I would ask you to read* Hind Swaraj *with my eyes and see therein the chapter on how to make India nonviolent. You cannot build nonviolence on factory civilization, but it can be built on self-contained villages."*[2]

Two of his last pronouncements on *Hind Swaraj* need to be extensively quoted. Both of them are in the form of letters. In a letter to one Mr. Krishnachandra on 14 June, 1945, he wrote:

"I still abide by whatever I wrote about railways, etc., in Hind Swaraj. *But that applies to be an ideal state. It is possible that we may never reach that state. Let us not worry about it. It is for this reason that I have said that if we do not feel unhappy. At the same time, we should also not make a duty of giving up these things. We should have a free and easy attitude in such matters. We must use these facilities as little as possible. There will be all types of people in the society. There certainly are today. We have to live with them. Non-attachment is the only proper* dharma *under these circumstances. The only thing we must be careful about is that we do not deceive ourselves. Your statement that trains, etc., should shunned, even as theft, adultery and falsehood, is not correct. The important reason for this is that even society considers theft, etc., to be immoral. Trains, etc., have not been, nor need they be so considered. All that we may say is that we should not consider trains, etc., as means of enjoyment."*[3]

1. *CWMG*, Vol. 70, p. 242.
2. *Ibid.*, p. 296.
3. *CWMG*, Vol. 80, p. 325.

The last letter he wrote was to Jawaharlal Nehru in which he explicitly referred to *Hind Swaraj*. "*I have said*", he wrote, that "*I fully stand by the kind of governance I have described in* Hind Swaraj...*My experience has confirmed the truth of what I wrote in 1909*."[1] Then he went on:

"*It is better that I redraw the picture today in my own language... What is worth knowing is only what I have to say today. I believe that if India, and through India the world, is to achieve freedom, than sooner or later we shall have to go and live in village—in huts, not in palaces. Millions of people can never live in cities and palaces in comfort and peace... We can have the vision of that truth and nonviolence only in the simplicity of the villages. That simplicity resides in the spinning wheel and what is implied by the spinning wheel... The sum and substance of what I want to say is that the individual person should have control over the things that are necessary for the sustenance of life*."[2]

One can analyse from the above statements that Gandhi's own evaluation of *Hind Swaraj* has undergone a change.

Methodology

In studying *Hind Swaraj*, the first problem that confronts a student is that of methodology. Is *Hind Swaraj* to be taken as a final blueprint, which the Mahatma was trying to realize in reconstructing the Indian society? Or, is it outburst of an Indian disgusted with the ills of modern civilization and its institutions, e.g., parliament, etc.? Or, is it a message that calls for rethinking of the entire approach of linear progress, which was the hallmark of the nineteenth and early twentieth centuries?[3]

All these questions are immediately arise as soon as one goes through the *Hind Swaraj*. To understand *Hind Swaraj* both with reference to India and the world at large, we will have to put the tract in a historical perspective. But before we do so, a word about the methodology of studying it is called for.[4]

1. *CWMG*, Vol. 81, p. 319.
2. *CWMG*, Vol. 81, pp. 319-20.
3. Nageshwar Prasad, *op. cit.*, p. 12.
4. *Ibid.*

From the point of view of methodology, *Hind Swaraj* cannot be tak en to be the final blueprint along which Gandhi wanted to refashion Indian society as well as the world order. *Hind Swaraj* "has reference to an ideal state." "Gandhiraj was an ideal condition," and he warned the reader "against thinking that I am today aiming at the *swaraj* described therein."[1]

One can see that Gandhi had a flexible mind. Yet from the series of citations, which we have mentioned above, it is clearly visible that the Mahatma was not willing to yield ground on the ideas propounded in the booklet. In the letter written to Nehru, which perhaps suggests his latest thinking, he said he fully stood by the kind of governance he described in *Hind Swaraj* and went on to say, "what is worth knowing is only what I have to say today." And then he proceeded to redraw the picture that he had in mind.[2]

It will appear, therefore, that the Mahatma expresses apparently contradictory opinions, which, it is assumed in some quarters, persisted till the end. Yet in Gandhi's own words:

> "I am not at all concerned with appearing to be consistent. In my search after truth, I have discarded many ideas and learnt many new things. Old as I am in age, I have no feeling that I have ceased to grow inwardly or that my growth will stop at the dissolution of my flesh. What I am concerned with is my readiness to obey the call of Truth, my God, from moment to moment, and, therefore, when anybody finds any inconsistency between any two writings of mine...he would do well to choose the latter of the two on the same subject."[3]

And Mahadev Desai very aptly expressed this when he said that while *"the views expressed in the first edition of* Hind Swaraj *have remained in substance unchanged, they have gone through a necessary evolution."*[4]

---

1. *Ibid.*
2. *Ibid.*, pp. 12-13.
3. *CWMG*, Vol. 55, p. 61.
4. M.K. Gandhi, *op.cit.*, p. 5.

This only means that there are some very basic and fundamental propositions on which Gandhi tried to build up what he called the whole theory of life. These basics remained unchanged and unmodified. In response to challenges posed to him by the limitations with which both the 'individual' man and the 'social situation' were constrained, he was willing to compromise on details.[1] Explore the fundamental propositions of Gandhi right from *Hind Swaraj* until his death in 1948. What we are aiming at is to show that while the basic model he conceived remained the same in working it out it was open to adaptation.

Studies on Hind Swaraj

Not until 1919, *Hind Swaraj* became widely known in intellectual circles in India. All of them, however, did not like it. S.A. Dange, a noted Communist leader, in his book *Gandhi* versus *Lenin* (1921) and M.N. Roy in his book *India in Transition* (1922) dismissed it as mere humanitarianism based on ignorance of the laws of class struggle. It is quite another thing that at least Dange changed his views so enormously in the later stages of his life that he almost became a Gandhian. Sir Shankar Nair, a leading lawyer of India (he was also the president of Indian National Congress) in his book *Gandhi and Anarchy* (1922), castigated Gandhi for advocating anarchism through *Satyagraha.*

Gandhi's *Hind Swaraj,* which contains his seminal ideas and basic approach to the problems of contemporary civilization, has not received the attention it merits. It is notable that during the period 1920-1947, when Gandhi dominated the national movement, the book *Hind Swaraj* was widely ignored. Even the intellectual community in the universities and in other centres of learning, research and public education did not evince much interest in *Hind Swaraj.* We know of only five major studies. Firstly, in 1938, Sophia Wadia devoted an entire issue of *Aryan Path* (London) to *Hind Swaraj.* Secondly, T.K. Mahadevan in 1973 brought out a special number of *Gandhi*

1. Nageshwar Prasad, p. 13.

Marg (New Delhi) on *Hind Swaraj*. Thirdly, Nageshwar Prasad brought a book entitled *Hind Swaraj : A Fresh Look* in 1985. Fourthly, Anthony J. Parel brought a book entitled *Gandhi: Hind Swaraj and Other Writings* in 1997. And recently Prof. R.P. Misra made a deep study of *Hind Swaraj* in 2006.

Summing Up

Hind Swaraj is one of the most significant treatises that Gandhi wrote to clarify his views. *Hind Swaraj* is perhaps the most systematic exposition of Gandhi's ideas of state, society and nation. Although *Hind Swaraj* is an original tract, while writing it Gandhi was heavily influenced by some of the leading Western thinkers[1] as well as Indian philosophy. It contains a statement of some of the fundamental tenets in Gandhi's politics. In other words, Gandhi stated his position quite clearly in *Hind Swaraj* and held onto it all his life. In fact, *Hind Swaraj* laid the most crucial theoretical foundation of his entire strategy for winning *swaraj* for India.[2] It is also the most authentic text of Gandhian social and political ideas dealing with *swaraj* and *satyagraha*. In *Hind Swaraj*, Gandhi depicted the dichotomies between the spiritual, moral fabric of Indian society, and the violent, politically corrupt nature of European states more dramatically than any of his predecessors.

The aim of *Hind Swaraj* was 'to confront the anarchist and violence-prone Indian nationalists with an alternative to violence, derived from Gandhi's earliest experiments with *satyagraha*'. *Hind Swaraj* served two purposes : on the one hand, it was a detailed commentary on Western civilization that thrived on naked force; it also laid down, on the other, the fundamental pillars later to become basic precepts of Gandhi's social and political ideas.[3]

Hind Swaraj is a foundational text for understanding Gandhi and his ideology. An outcome of a cross-fertilization of ideas, Indian and Western, *Hind Swaraj* was perhaps the most

1. Bidyut Chakarabarty, p. 23.
2. *Ibid.*
3. *Ibid.*, p. 24.

powerful exposition of Gandhian social and political ideas.[1] It is a significant text with refreshing ideas (a) critiquing the Western civilization; and also (b) seeking to build "a vernacular model of action" that the people of India understood.[2]

Gandhi's *Hind Swaraj* is not a rejection of the liberative contribution of modernity: civil liberties, religious tolerance, equality, poverty alleviation. Rather his effort can be interpreted as an attempt to integrate these positive elements with a liberating reinterpretation of tradition. With his critique from within the tradition, Gandhi becomes the great synthesizer of contraries within and across traditions.[3]

Hind Swaraj is a Gandhi's response to the immediate, contemporary problems arising out of inner and outer conflicts at individual, state and society level. *Hind Swaraj* also provides a vision, strategies, blueprint to future and an alternative to solve the contemporary problems. Future hope lies in *Hind Swaraj*.

Hind Swaraj is echoed in recent well-known studies like—*The Ages of Gaia* by James Lovelock; *The Turning Point* by Fritjof Capra; *Entropy: New Worldview* of Jeremy Refkin; *Human Destiny* by Lecompte du Nouy; *Clash of Civilization* by S.P. Huntington; *The Third Wave* by Elwin Toffler; *Deschooling Society* by Evan Ellich and *Mega Trends* by John Naisbistt. It is high time for both our policy makers and the people, to turn the torch within so that they may be inspired to adopt the way shown in *Hind Swaraj,* if not for any other consideration, but for its pragmatic strength to solve our present day maladies of India as well as of the whole world.

---

1. *Ibid.*
2. *Ibid.*
3. Rudolf C. Heredia, "Interpreting Gandhi's Hind Swaraj", *Economic and Political Weekly,* Vol. XXXIV, No. 24, June 12-18, 1999, p. 1501.

PART TWO

HIND SWARAJ OR INDIAN HOME RULE BY M.K. GANDHI

"HIND SWARAJ"[1]

Preface

I have written some[2] chapters on the subject of Indian Home

1. This was originally written in Gujarati during Gandhiji's return journey from England on the *Kildonan Castle* and published in *Indian Opinion*, the first twelve chapters on 11-12-1909 and the rest on 18-12-1909. Issued as a booklet in January 1910, it was proscribed in India by the Government of Bombay on March 24, 1910; *vide* "Our Publications", (7-5-1910). This hastened Gandhiji's decision to publish the English translation; *vide* "Preface to *Hind Swaraj*", (20-3-1910). This was issued by the International Printing Press, Phoenix, with a foreword by Gandhiji dated March 20, 1910 and also the English translation of the Gujarati foreword dated November 22, 1909, reproduced here.
   The text adopted here is that of the Revised New Edition published in 1939 by the Navajivan Press, Ahmedabad. Their first edition appeared in 1938 with a preface by Mahadev Desai, who also wrote (in the *Harijan*, 10-9-1938) an article on the *Hind Swaraj* Special Number of *The Aryan Path* (September 1938). This article of Desai's and a message from Gandhiji dated July 14, 1938 were included in the 1939 edition, the proofs of which had been, as Mahadev Desai states in his introductory lines dated December 11, 1938, "revised by numerous friends". Gandhiji discusses *Hind Swaraj* in the article "The Unbridgeable Gulf", *Harijan*, 14-10-1939.
   Ganesh & Co., Madras, brought out the first Indian edition in 1919 with Gandhiji's foreword dated May 28, 1919. Their fourth edition came out in 1921 with Gandhiji's article *"Hind Swaraj* or Indian Home Rule" in *Young India*, 26-1-1921. Their sixth edition was issued in 1924. In the same year appeared an American edition by H. T. Mazumdar with the title *Sermon on the Sea*.
   The second Gujarati edition was issued in May 1914, in South Africa, with a new Preface by Gandhiji, published in *Indian Opinion*, 29-4-1914. The Navajivan Press published in September 1923 a facsimile edition of the Gujarati original in Gandhiji's hand.
   Significant variations between the Revised New Edition of 1939 and the Gujarati original published in *Indian Opinion* in December 1909 are indicated in the footnotes.
2. "Twenty", according to the original Preface in Gujarati.

Rule which I venture to place before the readers of *Indian Opinion.* I have written because I could not restrain myself. I have read much, I have pondered much, during the stay, for four months[1] in London, of the Transvaal Indian deputation.[2] I discussed things with as many of my countrymen as I could. I met, too, as many Englishmen as it was possible for me to meet. I consider it my duty now to place before the readers of *Indian Opinion* the conclusions, which appear to me to be final. The Gujarati subscribers of *Indian Opinion* number about 800. I am aware that, for every subscriber, there are at least ten persons who read the paper with zest. Those who cannot read Gujarati have the paper read out to them. Such persons have often questioned me about the condition of India. Similar questions were addressed to me in London. I felt, therefore, that it might not be improper for me to ventilate publicly the views expressed by me in private.

These views are mine, and yet not mine. They are mine because I hope to act according to them. They are almost a part of my being. But, yet, they are not mine, because I lay no claim to originality. They have been formed after reading several books. That which I dimly felt received support from these books.[3]

The views I venture to place before the reader are, needless to say, held by many Indians not touched by what is known as civilization, but I ask the reader to believe me when I tell him that they are also held by thousands of Europeans. Those who wish to dive deep, and have time, may read certain books themselves. If time permits me, I hope to translate portions of such books for the benefit of the readers of *Indian Opinion.*

If the readers of *Indian Opinion* and others who may see the following chapters will pass their criticism on to me, I shall feel obliged to them.

1. July 10 to November 13.
2. The original has: "I have read much, I have pondered much. Also, during my four months' stay in London in connection with the work of the Transvaal Indian Deputation I discussed."
3. *Vide* "Some Authcrities", Appendix I to *Hind Swaraj.*

The only motive is to serve my country, to find out the Truth, and to follow it. If, therefore, my views are proved to be wrong, I shall have no hesitation in rejecting them. If they are proved to be right, I would naturally wish, for the sake of the motherland, that others should adopt them.

To make it easy reading, the chapters are written in the form of a dialogue between the reader and the editor.

KILDONAN CASTLE **Mohandas Karamchand Gandhi**
22-11-1909

1

The Congress and its Officials

Reader : Just at present there is a Home Rule wave passing over India. All our countrymen appear to be pinning for National Independence. A similar spirit pervades them even in South Africa. Indians seem to be eager to acquire rights. Will you explain your views in this matter?

Editor : You have put the question well, but the answer is not easy. One of the objects of a newspaper is to understand popular feeling and to give expression to it; another is to arouse among the people certain desirable sentiments; and the third is fearlessly to expose popular defects.[1] The exercise of all these three functions is involved in answering your question. To a certain extent the people's will has to be expressed, certain sentiments will need to be fostered, and defects will have to be brought to light.[2] But, as you have asked the question, it is my duty to answer it.

Reader : Do you then consider that a desire for Home Rule has been created among us ?

Editor : That desire gave rise to the National Congress.[3] The choice of the word "National" implies it.

Reader : That, surely, is not the case. Young India seems to ignore the Congress. It is considered to be an instrument for perpetuating British Rule.

1. The original adds: "whatever the difficulties in the way".
2. The original has: "and the defects will have to be condemned".
3. The original has: "That has been evident since the National Congress was established."

Editor : That opinion is not justified. Had not the Grand Old Man[1] of India prepared the soil, our young men could not have even spoken about Home Rule. How can we what Mr. Hume[2] has written, how he has lashed us into action, and with what effort he has awakened us, in order to achieve the objects of the Congress? Sir William Wedderburn[3] has given his body, mind and money to the same cause. His writings[4] are worthy of perusal to this day. Professor Gokhale[5] in order to prepare the nation, embraced poverty and gave twenty years of his life. Even now, he is living in poverty. The late Justice Budruddin Tyebji[6] was also one of those who, through the Congress, sowed the seed of Home Rule. Similarly, in Bengal, Madras, the Punjab and other places, there have been lovers of India and members of the Congress, both Indian and English.

Reader : Stay, stay; you are going too far, you are straying away from my question. I have asked you about Home or Self-Rule; you are discussing foreign rule. I do not desire to hear English names, and you are giving me such names. In these circumstances, I do not think we can ever meet. I shall be pleased if you will confine yourself to Home Rule. All other talk[7] will not satisfy me.

Editor : You are impatient. I cannot afford to be likewise. If you will bear with me for a while, I think you will find that you will obtain what you want. Remember the old proverb that the tree does not grow in one day. The fact that you have checked me and that you do not want to hear about the well-wishers of India shows that, for you at any rate, Home Rule is

1. Dadabhai Naoroji (1825-1917), *vide* Vol. II, p. 377; also vide "The Grand Old Man of India", p.313.
2. A.O. Hume, one of the founders of the Indian National Congress.
3. President, Indian National Congress at Bombay (1889) and at Allahabad (1910); *vide* Vol. I, p.386.
4. The original adds: "on British rule".
5. Distinguished Indian leader and statesman, educationist and reformer; *vide* Vol. II, pp. 377-8.
6 Judge of the Bombay High Court and President of the Indian National Congress at Madras (1887); *vide* Vol. IV, p. 442, footnote.
7. The original has: "This fine talk about other things will not satisfy me." The first Indian edition had: "All other wise talk. . ."

yet far away. If we had many like you, we would never make any advance. This thought is worthy of your attention.

Reader : It seems to me that you simply want to put me off by talking round and round. Those whom you consider to be well wishers of India are not such in my estimation. Why, then, should I listen to your discourse on such people?[1] What has he whom you consider to be the Father of the Nation done for it ? He says that the English Governors will do justice and that we should co-operate with them.

Editor : I must tell you, with all gentleness that it must be a matter of shame for us that you should speak about that great man in terms of disrespect. Just look at his work. He has dedicated his life to the service of India. We have learned what we know from him. It was the respected Dadabhai who taught us that the English had sucked our life-blood. What does it matter that, today, his trust is still in the English nation? Is Dadabhai less to be honoured because, in the exuberance of youth, we are prepared to go a step further? Are we, on that account, wiser than he? It is a mark of wisdom not to kick away the very step from which we have risen higher. The removal[2] of a step from a staircase brings down the whole of it. When, out of infancy, we grow into youth, we do not despise infancy, but on the contrary, we recall with affection the days of our childhood. If, after many years of study, a teacher were to teach me something, and if I were to build a little more on the foundation laid by that teacher, I would not, on that account, be considered wiser than the teacher. He would always command my respect. Such is the case with the Grand Old Man of India. We must admit that he is the author of nationalism.[3]

Reader : You have spoken well. I can now understand that we must look upon Mr. Dadabhai with respect. Without him and men like him, we should probably not have the spirit that fires us. How can the same be said of Professor Gokhale? He has constituted himself a great friend of the English; he

1. The original has: "Whose services, then, must I hear about?"
2. The original has: "It must be remembered that the removal."
3. The original has: "that he gave a lead to the Indian people".

says that we have to learn a great deal from them, that we have to learn their political wisdom, before we can talk of Home Rule. I am tired of reading his speeches.

Editor : If you are tired, it only betrays your impatience. We believe that those, who are discontented with the slowness of their parents and are angry because the parents would not run with their children, are considered disrespectful to their parents. Professor Gokhale occupies the place of a parent. What does it matter if he cannot run with us? A nation that is desirous of securing Home Rule cannot afford to despise its ancestors. We shall become useless, if we lack respect for our elders. Only men with mature thoughts are capable of ruling themselves and not the hasty-tempered. Moreover, how many Indians were there like Professor Gokhale, when he gave himself to Indian education? I verily believe that whatever Professor Gokhale does, he does with pure motives and with a view to serving India. His devotion to the Motherland is so great that he would give his life for it, if necessary. Whatever he says is said not to flatter anyone but because he believes it to be true. We are bound, therefore, to entertain the highest regard for him.

Reader : Are we, then, to follow him in every respect?

Editor : I never said any such thing. If we conscientiously differed from him, the learned Professor himself would advise us to follow the dictates of our conscience rather than him. Our chief purpose is not to decry his work, but to believe that he is infinitely greater than we are, and to feel assured that compared with his work for India, ours is infinitesimal. Several newspapers write disrespectfully of him. It is our duty to protest against such writings.We should consider men like Professor Gokhale to be the pillars of Home Rule. It is a bad habit to say that another man's thoughts are bad and ours only are good and that those holding different views from ours are the enemies of the country.

Reader : I now begin to understand somewhat your meaning. I shall have to think the matter over. But what you say about Mr. Hume and Sir William Wedderburn is beyond my comprehension.

Editor : The same rule holds good for the English as for the Indians. I can never subscribe to the statement that all Englishmen are bad. Many Englishmen desire Home Rule for India. That the English people are somewhat more selfish than others is true, but that does not prove that every Englishman is bad. We who seek justice will have to do justice to others. Sir William does not wish ill to India—that should be enough for us. As we proceed, you will see that, if we act justly, India will be sooner free. You will see, too, that if we shun every Englishman as an enemy, Home Rule will be delayed. But if we are just to them, we shall receive their support in our progress towards the goal.

Reader : All this seems to me at present to be simply nonsensical. English support and the obtaining of Home Rule are two contradictory things. How can the English people tolerate Home Rule for us? But I do not want you to decide this question for me just yet. To spend time over it is useless. When you have shown how we can have Home Rule, perhaps I shall understand your views. You have prejudiced me against you by discoursing on English help. I would, therefore, beseech you not to continue this subject.

Editor : I have no desire to do so. That you are prejudiced against me is not a matter for much anxiety. It is well that I should say unpleasant things at the commencement. It is my duty patiently to try to remove your prejudice.

Reader : I like that last statement. It emboldens me to say what I like. One thing still puzzles me. I do not understand how the Congress laid the foundation of Home Rule.

Editor : Let us see. The Congress brought together Indians from different parts of India, and enthused us with the idea of nationality. The Government used to look upon it with disfavour. The Congress has always insisted that the Nation should control revenue and expenditure. It has always desired self-government after the Canadian model. Whether we can get it or not, whether we desire it or not, and whether there is not something more desirable, are different questions. All I have to show is that the Congress gave us a foretaste of Home

Rule. To deprive it of the honour is not proper,[1] and for us to do so would not only be ungrateful, but retard the fulfilment of our object. To treat the Congress[2] as an institution inimical to our growth as a nation would disable us from using that body.

1. The original has: "It would be improper for others to claim that honour...."
2. The original has: "To dissociate ourselves from the Congress and treat it...."

2

The Partition of Bengal

Reader : Considering the matter as you put it, it seems proper to say that the foundation of Home Rule was laid by the Congress. But you will admit that this cannot be considered a real awakening. When and how did the real awakening take place?

Editor : The seed is never seen. It works underneath the ground, is itself destroyed, and the tree which rises above the ground is alone seen. Such is the case with the Congress. Yet, what you call the real awakening took place after the Partition of Bengal. For this we have to be thankful to Lord Curzon[1] . At the time of the Partition,[2] the people of Bengal reasoned with Lord Curzon, but in the pride of power he disregarded all their prayers. He took it for granted that Indians could only prattle, that they could never take any effective steps. He used insulting language, and in the teeth of all opposition partitioned Bengal. That day may be considered to be the day of the partition of the British Empire. The shock the British power received through the Partition has never been equalled by any other act. This does not mean that the other injustices done to India are less glaring than that done by the Partition. The salt tax is not a small injustice. We shall see many such things later on. But the people were ready to resist the Partition. At that time feeling ran high. Many leading Bengalis were ready to lose their all. They knew their power; hence the conflagration. It is

1. Viceroy of India, 1899-l905; *vide* Vol. V, pp. 47-48.
2. In 1905.

now well-nigh unquenchable; it is not necessary to quench it either. The Partition will go, Bengal will be reunited, but the rift in the English barque will remain; it must daily widen. India awakened is not likely to fall asleep. The demand for the abrogation of the Partition is tantamount to a demand for Home Rule. Leaders in Bengal know this. British officials realize it. That is why the Partition still remains. As time passes, the Nation is being forged. Nations are not formed in a day; the formation requires years.

Reader : What, in your opinion, are the results of the Partition?

Editor : Hitherto we have considered that for redress of grievances we must approach the throne, and if we get no redress we must sit still, except that we may still petition. After the Partition, people saw that petitions must be backed up by force, and that they must be capable of suffering. This new spirit must be considered to be the chief result of the Partition. That spirit was seen in the outspoken writings in the Press. That which the people said tremblingly and in secret began to be said and to be written publicly. The *Swadeshi* movement was inaugurated. People, young and old, used to run away at the sight of an English face; it now no longer awes them. They do not fear even a row, or being imprisoned. Some of the best sons of India are at present in banishment.[1] This is something different from mere petitioning. Thus are the people moved. The spirit generated in Bengal has spread in the north to the Punjab, and in the south to Cape Comorin.

Reader : Do you suggest any other striking result?

Editor : The Partition has not only made a rift in the English ship but has made it in ours also. Great events always produce great results. Our leaders are divided into two parties: the Moderates and the Extremists. These may be considered as the slow party and the impatient party. Some call the Moderates the timid party, and the Extremists the bold party. All interpret the two words according to their preconceptions.

1. Bal Gangadhar Tilak, the Father of Indian Unrest, was in Mandalay prison at this time.

This much is certain—that there has arisen an enmity between the two. The one distrusts the other and imputes motives. At the time of the Surat Congress[1] there was almost a fight. I think that this division is not a good thing for the country, but I think also that such divisions will not last long. It all depends upon the leaders how long they will last.

1. In 1907.

3

Discontent and Unrest

Reader : Then you consider the Partition to be a cause of the awakening? Do you welcome the unrest which has resulted from it?

Editor : When a man rises from sleep, he twists his limbs and is restless. It takes some time before he is entirely awakened. Similarly, although the Partition has caused an awakening, the comatose condition has not yet disappeared. We are still twisting our limbs and are still restless, and just as the state between sleep and awakening must be considered to be necessary, so may the present unrest in India be considered a necessary and, therefore, a proper state. The knowledge that there is unrest will, it is highly probable, enable us to outgrow it. Rising from sleep, we do not continue in a comatose state, but according to our ability, sooner or later, we are completely restored to our senses. So shall we be free from the present unrest which no one likes.

Reader : What is the other form of unrest ?

Editor : Unrest is, in reality, discontent. The latter is only now described as unrest. During the Congress period, it was labelled discontent. Mr. Hume always said that the spread of discontent in India was necessary. This discontent is a very useful thing. As long as a man is contented with his present lot, so long is it difficult to persuade him to come out of it. Therefore, it is that every reform must be preceded by discontent. We throw away things we have, only when we cease to like them. Such discontent has been produced among us after reading the great works of Indians and Englishmen.

Discontent has led to unrest, and the latter has brought about many deaths,[1] many imprisonments, many banishments.[2] Such a state of things will still continue. It must be so. All these may be considered good signs but they may also lead to bad results.

---

1. The original adds here: "many flights...."
2. Gandhiji must have had in mind the assassination of Englishmen and Indians by terrorists, who were sentenced to death or deportation or long terms of imprisonment. In 1908, Mrs. and Miss Kennedy were killed by Khudi Ram Bose, a youngster of 18, who had flung a bomb at Kingsford, the District Magistrate of Muzaffarpur in Bengal and missed him. Sub-Inspector Nandlal, who had arrested Khudi Ram Bose, was murdered, as also Narendra Gosain, approver in the Alipore Conspiracy Case, in which Aurobindo Ghosh, defended by C. R. Das, who had earlier defended B. C. Pal in sedition cases, was acquitted, in 1909, but many others were awarded heavy sentences including transportation for life. In 1909, Ganesh Savarkar was sentenced to transportation for life on a charge of writing inflammatory verses; and Ashutosh Biswas, Public Prosecutor, was shot dead, while leaving the court in Calcutta. On July 1, a few days before Gandhiji reached London, Madan Lal Dhingra had shot dead Sir Curzon Wyllie in London. Among the banishments were those in 1907 of Lala Lajpatrai and Ajit Singh of Punjab and of B. G. Tilak who was in prison in Mandalay from 1908 to 1914.

4

What is Swaraj?

Reader : I have now learnt what the Congress has done to make India one nation, how the Partition has caused an awakening, and how discontent and unrest have spread through the land. I would now like to know your views on *Swaraj.* I fear that our interpretation is not the same as yours.

Editor : It is quite possible that we do not attach the same meaning to the term. You and I and all Indians are impatient to obtain *Swaraj,* but we are certainly not decided as to what it is. To drive the English out of India is a thought heard from many mouths, but it does not seem that many have properly considered why it should be so. I must ask you a question. Do you think that it is necessary to drive away the English, if we get all we want?

Reader : I should ask of them only one thing, that is: "Please leave our country." If, after they have complied with this request, their withdrawal from India means[1] that they are still in India, I should have no objection. Then we would understand that, in their language, the word "gone" is equivalent to "remained".

Editor : Well then, let us suppose that the English have retired. What will you do then ?

Reader : That question cannot be answered at this stage. The state after withdrawal will depend largely upon the manner of it. If, as you assume, they retire, it seems to me we shall still keep their constitution and shall carry on the Government. If they simply retire for the asking, we should

1. The original has: "is taken to mean, perversely enough."

have an army, etc., ready at hand. We should, therefore, have no difficulty in carrying on the Government.

Editor : You may think so; I do not. But I will not discuss the matter just now. I have to answer your question, and that I can do well by asking you several questions. Why do you want to drive away the English?

Reader : Because India has become impoverished by their Government. They take away our money from year to year. The most important posts are reserved for themselves. We are kept in a state of slavery. They behave insolently towards us and disregard our feelings.

Editor : If they do not take our money away, become gentle, and give us responsible posts, would you still consider their presence to be harmful?

Reader : That question is useless. It is similar to the question whether there is any harm in associating with a tiger if he changes his nature. Such a question is sheer waste of time. When a tiger changes his nature, Englishmen will change theirs. This is not possible, and to believe it to be possible is contrary to human experience.[1]

Editor : Supposing we get Self-Government similar to what the Canadians and the South Africans[2] have, will it be good enough?

Reader : That question also is useless. We may get it when we have the same powers;[3] we shall then hoist our own flag. As is Japan, so must India be. We must own our navy, our army, and we must have our own splendour, and then will India's voice ring through the world.

Editor : You have drawn the picture well. In effect it means this: that we want English rule without the Englishman. You want the tiger's nature, but not the tiger; that is to say, you would make India English. And when it becomes English, it will be called not Hindustan but *Englistan*. This is not the *Swaraj* that I want.

---

1. The original has: "and it is certainly absurd of a man to believe that the impossible will be possible."
2. The original has: "Boers".
3. The original has: "when we have firearms in the same way that they have".

Reader : I have placed before you my idea of *Swaraj* as I think it should be. If the education we have received be of any use, if the works of Spencer, Mill and others be of any importance, and if the English Parliament be the Mother of Parliaments, I certainly think that we should copy the English people, and this to such an extent that, just as they do not allow others to obtain a footing in their country, so we should not allow them or others to obtain it in ours. What they have done in their own country has not been done in any other country. It is, therefore, proper for us to import their institutions. But now I want to know your views.

Editor : There is need for patience. My views will develop of themselves in the course of this discourse. It is as difficult for me to understand the true nature of *Swaraj* as it seems to you to be easy. I shall, therefore, for the time being, content myself with endeavouring to show that what you call *Swaraj* is not truly *Swaraj*.

5

The Condition of England

Reader : Then from your statement I deduce that the Government of England is not desirable[1] and not worth copying by us.

Editor : Your deduction is justified. The condition of England at present is pitiable. I pray to God that India may never be in that plight. That which you consider to be the Mother of Parliaments is like a sterile woman and a prostitute. Both these are harsh terms, but exactly fit the case. That Parliament has not yet, of its own accord, done a single good thing. Hence, I have compared it to a sterile woman. The natural condition of that Parliament is such that, without outside pressure, it can do nothing. It is like a prostitute because it is under the control of ministers who change from time to time. Today it is under Mr. Asquith[2], tomorrow it may be under Mr. Balfour[3].

Reader : You have said this sarcastically. The term "sterile woman" is not applicable. The Parliament, being elected by the people, must work under public pressure. This is its quality.[4]

1. The original has: ". . . the Government which England enjoys is not the right kind and . . . ."
2. Herbert Henry Asquith (1852-1928), Prime Minister of Great Britain, 1908-16
3. Arthur James Balfour, Prime Minister of Great Britain, 1902-05. The original adds: "and the day after, it will be somebody else".
4. The original has: "That is its very nature, what keeps it in check."

Editor : You are mistaken. Let us examine it a little more closely.[1] The best men are supposed to be elected by the people. The members serve without pay[2] and therefore, it must be assumed, only for the public weal. The electors are considered to be educated and, therefore, we should assume that they would not generally make mistakes in their choice. Such a Parliament should not need the spur of petitions or any other pressure. Its work should be so smooth that its effects would be more apparent day by day. But, as a matter of fact, it is generally acknowledged that the members are hypocritical and selfish. Each thinks of his own little interest. It is fear that is the guiding motive. What is done today may be undone tomorrow. *It is not possible to recall a single instance in which finality can be predicted for its work*. When the greatest questions are debated, its members have been seen to stretch themselves and to doze. Sometimes the members talk away until the listeners are disgusted. Carlyle has called it the "talking shop of the world". Members vote for their party without a thought. Their so-called discipline binds them to it. If any member, by way of exception, gives an independent vote, he is considered a renegade. If the money and the time wasted by Parliament were entrusted to a few good men, the English nation would be occupying today a much higher platform. Parliament is simply a costly toy of the nation. These views are by no means peculiar to me. Some great English thinkers have expressed them. One of the members of that Parliament recently said that a true Christian could not become a member of it. Another said that it was a baby. And if it has remained a baby after an existence of seven hundred years, when will it outgrow its babyhood?

Reader : You have set me thinking; you do not expect me to accept at once all you say. You give me entirely novel views. I shall have to digest them. Will you now explain the epithet "prostitute" ?

---

1. The original has: "If Parliament were not like a sterile woman, this is what we might expect."
2. Payment to members began in 1911.

Editor : That you cannot accept my views at once is only right. If you will read the literature on this subject, you will have some idea of it.[1] Parliament is without a real master.[2] Under the Prime Minister,[3] its movement is not steady but it is buffeted about like a prostitute. The Prime Minister is more concerned about his power than about the welfare of Parliament. His energy is concentrated upon securing the success of his party. His care is not always that Parliament shall do right. Prime Ministers are known to have made Parliament do things merely for party advantage. All this is worth thinking over.

Reader : Then you are really attacking the very men whom we have hitherto considered to be patriotic and honest?

Editor : Yes, that is true; I can have nothing against Prime Ministers, but what I have seen leads me to think that they cannot be considered really patriotic. If they are to be considered honest because they do not take what are generally known as bribes, let them be so considered, but they are open to subtler influences. In order to gain their ends, they certainly bribe people with honours. I do not hesitate to say that they have neither real honesty nor a living conscience.

Reader : As you express these views about Parliament, I would like to hear you on the English people, so that I may have your view of their Government.

---

1. The original adds: "The description of Parliament as a prostitute is also justified." It is this sentence which probably Gandhiji had in mind when he said later in his preface, dated 28-5-1919, to *Hind Swaraj* published by Ganesh & Co.: "I have re-read this booklet more than once. The value at the present moment lies in reprinting it as it is. But if I had to revise it, there is only one word I would alter in accordance with a promise made to an English friend. She took exception to my use of the word 'prostitute' in speaking of the Parliament. Her fine taste recoiled from the indelicacy of the expression."
2. The original adds: "It cannot be under one master all the time. But this is not all that I mean."
3. The original has: "Even when a person becomes its master—say, the Prime Minister—it is not loyal to him all the time. Its ways are always the ways of a prostitute."

Editor : To the English voters their newspaper is their Bible. They take their cue from their newspapers which are often dishonest. The same fact is differently interpreted by different newspapers, according to the party in whose interests they are edited.[1] One newspaper would consider a great Englishman to be a paragon of honesty, another would consider him dishonest. What must be the condition of the people whose newspapers are of this type?

Reader : You shall describe it.

Editor : These people change their views frequently. It is said that they change them every seven years. These views swing like the pendulum of a clock and are never steadfast. The people would follow a powerful orator or a man[2] who gives them parties, receptions, etc. As are the people, so is their Parliament. They have certainly one quality very strongly developed. They will never allow their country to be lost. If any person were to cast an evil eye on it, they would pluck out his eyes. But that does not mean that the nation possesses every other virtue or that it should be imitated. If India copies England, it is my firm conviction that she will be ruined.

Reader : To what do you ascribe this state of England?

Editor : It is not due to any peculiar fault of the English people, but the condition is due to modern civilization. It is a civilization only in name. Under it the nations of Europe are becoming degraded and ruined day by day.

---

1. The original has: "one party magnifying its importance and the other minimising it".
2. The original has: "join the bandwagon of any powerful orator or man...."

6

Civilization

Reader : Now you will have to explain what you mean by civilization.[1]

Editor : It is not a question of what I mean. Several English writers refuse to call that civilization which passes under that name. Many books have been written upon that subject. Societies have been formed to cure the nation of the evils of civilization. A great English writer[2] has written a work called *Civilization : Its Cause and Cure*. Therein he has called it a disease.

Reader : Why do we not know this generally?

Editor : The answer is very simple. We rarely find people arguing against themselves. Those who are intoxicated by modern civilization are not likely to write against it. Their care will be to find out facts and arguments in support of it, and this they do unconsciously, believing it to be true. A man, whilst he is dreaming, believes in his dream; he is undeceived only when he is awakened from his sleep. A man labouring under the bane of civilization is like a dreaming man. What we usually read are the works of defenders of modern civilization, which undoubtedly claims among its votaries very brilliant and even some very good men. Their writings hypnotize us. And so, one by one, we are drawn into the vortex.

Reader : This seems to be very plausible. Now will you tell me something of what you have read and thought of this civilization?

1. The original adds: "According to you, civilization is not civilization but the opposite of it."
2. Edward Carpenter; *vide* Appendix I to *Hind Swaraj*, p. 65.

Editor : Let us first consider what state of things is described by the word "civilization". Its true test lies in the fact that people living in it make bodily welfare the object of life. We will take some examples. The people of Europe today live in better-built houses than they did a hundred years ago. This is considered an emblem of civilization, and this is also a matter to promote bodily happiness.[1] Formerly, they wore skins, and used spears as their weapons. Now, they wear long trousers, and, for embellishing their bodies, they wear a variety of clothing, and, instead of spears, they carry with them revolvers containing five or more chambers.[2] If people of a certain country, who have hitherto not been in the habit of wearing much clothing, boots, etc., adopt European clothing, they are supposed to have become civilized out of savagery. Formerly, in Europe, people ploughed their lands mainly by manual labour. Now, one man can plough a vast tract by means of steam engines and can thus amass great wealth. This is called a sign of civilization. Formerly, only a few men wrote valuable books.[3] Now, anybody writes and prints anything he likes and poisons people's minds.[4] Formerly, men travelled in waggons.[5] Now, they fly through the air[6] in planes at the rate of four hundred and more miles per day. This is considered the height of civilization. It has been stated that, as men progress, they shall be able to travel in airships and reach any part of the world in a few hours. Men will not need the use of their hands and feet. They will press a button, and they will have their clothing by their side. They will press another button, and they will have their newspaper. A third, and a motor-car will be in waiting for them. They will have a variety of delicately dished up food. Everything will be done by machinery. Formerly,

1. The original has: " . . . an emblem of civilization. This is a matter which concerns physical comfort."
2. The original adds: "; that is considered a sign of civilization".
3. The original has: "Only a few men wrote books, and they were esteemed very highly."
4. The original adds: "; this is considered a sign of civilization".
5. The original adds: "covering about 20 miles in a day".
6. The words for "through the air" are not found in the Gujarati text.

when people wanted to fight with one another, they measured between them their bodily strength; now it is possible to take away thousands of lives by one man working behind a gun from a hill. This is civilization. Formerly, men worked in the open air only as much as they liked. Now thousands of workmen meet together and for the sake of maintenance work in factories or mines. Their condition is worse than that of beasts. They are obliged to work, at the risk of their lives, at most dangerous occupations, for the sake of millionaires.

Formerly, men were made slaves under physical compulsion. Now they are enslaved by temptation of money and of the luxuries that money can buy. There are now diseases of which people never dreamt before, and an army of doctors is engaged in finding out their cures, and so hospitals have increased. This is a test of civilization. Formerly, special messengers were required and much expense was incurred in order to send letters; today, anyone can abuse his fellow by means of a letter for one penny. True, at the same cost, one can send one's thanks also. Formerly, people had two or three meals consisting of home-made bread and vegetables; now, they require something to eat every two hours so that they have hardly leisure for anything else. What more need I say? All this you can ascertain from several authoritative books. These are all true tests of civilization.[1] And if anyone speaks to the contrary, know that he is ignorant.[2] This civilization takes note neither of morality nor of religion. Its votaries calmly state that their business is not to teach religion. Some even consider it to be a superstitious growth. Others put on the cloak of religion, and prate about morality. But, after twenty years' experience, I have come to the conclusion that immorality is often taught in the name of morality. Even a child can understand that in all I have described above there can be no inducement to morality. Civilization seeks to increase bodily comforts, and it fails miserably even in doing so.

---

1. The original has : "All these are indeed taken to be signs of civilization."
2. The original adds: "Civilization is what I have described it to be."

This civilization is irreligion, and it has taken such a hold on the people in Europe that those who are in it appear to be half mad. They lack real physical strength or courage. They keep up their energy by intoxication. They can hardly be happy in solitude. Women, who should be the queens of households, wander in the streets or they slave away in factories. For the sake of a pittance, half a million[1] women in England alone are labouring under trying circumstances[2] in factories or similar institutions. This awful fact is one of the causes of the daily growing[3] suffragette movement. This civilization is such that one has only to be patient and it will be self-destroyed. According to the teaching of Mahomed this would be considered a Satanic Civilization. Hinduism calls it the Black Age. I cannot give you an adequate conception of it.[4] It is eating into the vitals of the English nation.[5] It must be shunned.[6] Parliaments are really emblems of slavery. If you will sufficiently think over this, you will entertain the same opinion and cease to blame the English. They rather deserve our sympathy. They are a shrewd nation and I, therefore, believe that they will cast off the evil. They are enterprising and industrious, and their mode of thought is not inherently immoral. Neither are they bad at heart. I, therefore, respect them. Civilization is not an incurable disease,[7] but it should never be forgotten that the English people are at present afflicted by it.

---

1. The original has: "four million".
2. The original has: ". . . are labouring like beasts of burden".
3. The words for "awful" and "daily growing" are not found in the original.
4. The original adds: "That is beyond my capacity."
5. The original adds: "It is a deadly civilization, and is bound to perish."
6. The original adds: "These are the reasons why the British Parliament and other parliaments as well are found to be ineffective."
7. The original has: "It is not that they cannot be cured of this disease of civilization,. . . ."

7

Why was India Lost ?

Reader : You have said much about civilization—enough to make me ponder over it. I do not now know what I should adopt and what I should avoid from the nations of Europe, but one question comes to my lips immediately. If civilization is a disease[1] and if it has attacked England, why has she been able to take India, and why is she able to retain it?

Editor : Your question is not very difficult to answer, and we shall presently be able to examine the true nature of *Swaraj;* for I am aware that I have still to answer that question. I will, however, take up your previous question. The English have not taken India; we have given it to them. They are not in India because of their strength, but because we keep them. Let us now see whether these propositions can be sustained. They came to our country originally for purposes of trade. Recall the Company[2] *Bahadur*[3]. Who made it *Bahadur*? They had not the slightest intention at the time of establishing a kingdom. Who assisted the Company's officers? Who was tempted at the sight of their silver? Who bought their goods? History testifies that we did all this. In order to become rich all at once we welcomed the Company's officers with open arms. We assisted them. If I am in the habit of drinking *bhang* and a seller thereof sells it to me, am I to blame him or myself? By blaming the seller, shall I be able to avoid the habit? And, if a particular retailer is driven away, will not another take his place? A true

1. The original has: "If civilization is not civilization but the opposite of it, if it is a disease. . . ."
2. East India Company.
3. Literally, 'brave', here 'powerful', 'sovereign'.

servant of India will have to go to the root of the matter. If an excess of food has caused me indigestion, I shall certainly not avoid it by blaming water. He is a true physician who probes the cause of disease, and if you pose as a physician for the disease of India, you will have to find out its true cause.

Reader : You are right. Now I think you will not have to argue much with me to drive your conclusions home. I am impatient to know your further views. We are now on a most interesting topic. I shall, therefore, endeavour to follow your thought, and stop you when I am in doubt.

Editor : I am afraid that,[1] in spite of your enthusiasm, as we proceed further, we shall have differences of opinion. Nevertheless, I shall argue only when you stop me. We have already seen that the English merchants were able to get a footing in India because we encouraged them. When our Princes fought among themselves, they sought the assistance of Company Bahadur. That cooperation was versed alike in commerce and war. It was unhampered by questions of morality. Its object was to increase its commerce and to make money. It accepted our assistance, and increased the number of its warehouses. To protect the latter it employed an army which was utilized by us also. Is it not then useless to blame the English for what we did at that time? The Hindus and the Mahomedans were at daggers drawn. This, too, gave the Company its opportunity and thus we created the circumstances that gave the Company its control over India. Hence it is truer to say that we gave India to the English than that India was lost.

Reader : Will you now tell me how they are able to retain India?

Editor : The causes that gave them India enable them to retain it. Some Englishmen state that they took and they hold India by the sword. Both these statements are wrong. The sword is entirely useless for holding India. We alone keep them. Napoleon is said to have described the English as a nation of shop-keepers. It is a fitting description. They hold whatever

1. In the original, the paragraph begins: "Very well. I am afraid. . . ."

dominions they have for the sake of their commerce. Their army and their navy are intended to protect it. When the Transvaal offered no such attractions, the late Mr. Gladstone[1] discovered that it was not right for the English to hold it. When it became a paying proposition, resistance led to war. Mr. Chamberlain[2] soon discovered that England enjoyed a suzerainty over the Transvaal. It is related that someone asked the late President Kruger[3] whether there was gold in the moon. He replied that it was highly unlikely because, if there were, the English would have annexed it. Many problems can be solved by remembering that money is their God. Then it follows that we keep the English in India for our base self-interest. We like their commerce; they please us by their subtle methods and get what they want from us. To blame them for this is to perpetuate their power. We further strengthen their hold by quarrelling amongst ourselves. If you accept the above statements, it is proved that the English entered India for the purposes of trade. They remain in it for the same purpose and we help them to do so. Their arms and ammunition are perfectly useless. In this connection I remind you that it is the British flag which is waving in Japan and not the Japanese. The English have a treaty with Japan for the sake of their commerce, and you will see that if they can manage it, their commerce will greatly expand in that country. They wish to convert the whole world into a vast market for their goods. That they cannot do so is true, but the blame will not be theirs. They will leave no stone unturned to reach the goal.[4]

---

1. William Ewart Gladstone (1809-98), Prime Minister of Great Britain, 1868-74; 1880-85, 1886, and 1892-94.
2. Joseph Chamberlain (1836-1914), Secretary of State for the Colonies, 1895.
3. Stephanus Johannes Paulus Kruger (1825-1904), Boer leader and State President of the South African Republic; *vide* Vol.III, p. 66.
4. The original has : "They will not spare any effort."

8

I
The Condition of India

Reader : I now understand why the English hold India. I should like to know your views about the condition of our country.

Editor : It is a sad condition. In thinking of it my eyes water and my throat gets parched. I have grave doubts whether I shall be able sufficiently to explain what is in my heart. It is my deliberate opinion that India is being ground down, not under the English heel, but under that of modern civilization. It is groaning under the monster's terrible weight. There is yet time to escape it, but everyday makes it more and more difficult. Religion is dear to me and my first complaint is that India is becoming irreligious. Here I am not thinking of the Hindu or the Mahomedan or the Zoroastrian religion but of that religion which underlies all religions. We are turning away from God.

Reader : How so?

Editor : There is a charge laid against us that we are a lazy people and that Europeans are industrious and enterprising. We have accepted the charge and we, therefore, wish to change our condition. Hinduism, Islam, Zoroastrianism, Christianity and all other religions teach that we should remain passive about worldly pursuits and active about godly pursuits, that we should set a limit to our worldly ambition and that our religious ambition should be illimitable. Our activity should be directed into the latter channel.

Reader : You seem to be encouraging religious charlatanism. Many a cheat has, by talking in a similar strain, led the people astray.[1]

1. The original adds: "and still does so".

Editor : You are bringing an unlawful charge against religion. Humbug there undoubtedly is about all religions. Where there is light, there is also shadow. I am prepared to maintain that humbugs in worldly matters are far worse than the humbugs in religion. The humbug of civilization that I am endeavouring to show to you is not to be found in religion.

Reader : How can you say that? In the name of religion Hindus and Mahomedans fought against one another. For the same cause Christians fought Christians. Thousands of innocent men have been murdered, thousands have been burned and tortured in its name. Surely, this is much worse than any civilization.

Editor : I certainly submit that the above hardships are far more bearable than those of civilization. Everybody understands that the cruelties you have named are not part of religion although they have been practised in its name, therefore, there is no aftermath to these cruelties.[1] They will always happen so long as there are to be found ignorant and credulous people.[2]

But there is no end to the victims destroyed in the fire of civilization. Its deadly effect is that people come under its scorching flames believing it to be all good. They become utterly irreligious and, in reality, derive little advantage from the world.[3] Civilization is like a mouse gnawing while it is soothing us. When its full effect is realized, we shall see that religious superstition is harmless compared to that of modern civilization. I am not pleading for a continuance of religious superstitions. We shall certainly fight them tooth and nail, but we can never do so by disregarding religion. We can only do so by appreciating and conserving the latter.

Reader : Then you will contend that the Pax Britannica is a useless encumbrance ?

Editor : You may see peace if you like; I see none.

---

1. The original has: "; therefore they cease when their perpetrators die".
2. The original adds: "But their evil effects do not remain for ever".
3. Gujarati saying used by Gandhiji means: "They neither follow the way of religion nor that of the world." The original also adds: "They forget the things that really matter."

Reader : You make light of the terror that the Thugs[1], the Pindaris[2] and the Bhils[3] were to the country.

Editor : If you give the matter some thought, you will see that the terror was by no means such a mighty thing. If it had been a very substantial thing, the other people would have died away before the English advent. Moreover, the present peace is only nominal, for by it we have become emasculated and cowardly. We are not to assume that the English have changed the nature of the Pindaris and the Bhils. It is, therefore, better to suffer the Pindari peril than that someone else should protect us from it and thus render us effeminate. I should prefer to be killed by the arrow of a Bhil than to seek unmanly protection. India without such protection was an India full of valour. Macaulay betrayed gross ignorance when he libelled Indians as being practically cowards. They never merited the charge. Cowards living in a country inhabited by hardy mountaineers and infested by wolves and tigers must surely find an early grave. Have you ever visited our fields? I assure you that our agriculturists sleep fearlessly on their farms even today; but the English and you and I would hesitate to sleep where they sleep. Strength[4] lies in absence of fear, not in the quantity of flesh and muscle we may have on our bodies. Moreover, I must remind you who desire Home Rule that, after all, the Bhils, the Pindaris,[5] and the Thugs are our own countrymen. To conquer[6] them is your and my work. So long as we fear our own brethren, we are unfit to reach the goal.

1. Predatory groups that used to loot, rob and kill people.
2. Mounted marauders during the 17th and 18th centuries.
3. Tribe in Central India and Gujarat.
4. The original begins: "A little reflection will show that strength . . ."
5. The original adds: "the Assamese". This was, however, deleted in all subsequent editions.
6. The original has "To win them over".

9

II
The Condition of India (*Contd.*): *Railways*

Reader : You have deprived me of the consolation I used to have regarding peace in India.[1]

Editor : I have merely given you my opinion on the religious aspect, but when I give you my views as to the poverty of India, you will perhaps begin to dislike me because what you and I have hitherto considered beneficial for India no longer appears to me to be so.

Reader : What may that be ?

Editor : Railways, lawyers and doctors have impoverished the country so much so that, if we do not wake up in time, we shall be ruined.

Reader : I do now, indeed, fear that we are not likely to agree at all. You are attacking the very institutions which we have hitherto considered to be good.

Editor : It is necessary to exercise patience. The true inwardness of the evils of civilization you will understand with difficulty. Doctors assure us that a consumptive clings to life even when he is about to die. Consumption does not produce apparent hurt—it even produces a seductive colour about a patient's face so as to induce the belief that all is well.[2] Civilization is such a disease and we have to be very wary.[3]

---

1. The original has: "You have shattered my illusions about the value of peace in India." The original adds further: "You have left me with nothing that I can think of."
2. The original has: " . . . about a patient's face so that he keeps on hoping that all will be well, till he succumbs in the end".
3. The original has: "This is also true of civilization. It is a disease that cannot be detected. Be on your guard against it."

Reader : Very well, then. I shall hear you on the railways.

Editor : It must be manifest to you that, but for the railways, the English could not have such a hold on India as they have. The railways, too, have spread the bubonic plague. Without them, the masses could not move from place to place. They are the carriers of plague germs. Formerly, we had natural segregation. Railways have also increased the frequency of famines because, owing to facility of means of locomotion, people sell out their grain and it is sent to the dearest markets. People become careless and so the pressure of famine increases. Railways accentuate the evil nature of man. Bad men fulfil their evil designs with greater rapidity. The holy places of India have become unholy. Formerly, people went to these places with very great difficulty. Generally, therefore, only the real devotees visited such places. Now-a-days rogues visit them in order to practise their roguery.

Reader : You have given a one-sided account. Good men can visit these places as well as bad men. Why do they not take the fullest advantage of the railways?

Editor : Good travels at a snail's pace—it can, therefore, have little to do with the railways. Those who want to do good are not selfish, they are not in a hurry, they know that to impregnate people with good requires a long time. But evil has wings. To build a house takes time. Its destruction takes none. So the railways can become a distributing agency for the evil one only. It may be a debatable matter whether railways spread famines, but it is beyond dispute that they propagate evil.

Reader : Be that as it may, all the disadvantages of railways are more than counterbalanced by the fact that it is due to them that we see in India the new spirit of nationalism.

Editor : I hold this to be a mistake. The English have taught us that we were not one nation before and that it will require centuries before we become one nation. This is without foundation. We were one nation before they came to India. One thought inspired us. Our mode of life was the same. It was because we were one nation that they were able to establish one kingdom. Subsequently they divided us.

Reader : This requires an explanation.

Editor :[1] I do not wish to suggest that because we were one nation we had no differences, but it is submitted that our leading men travelled throughout India either on foot or in bullock-carts. They learned one another's languages and there was no aloofness between them. What do you think could have been the intention of those farseeing ancestors of ours who established Setubandha (Rameshwar) in the South, Jagannath in the East and Hardwar in the North as places of pilgrimage ? You will admit they were no fools. They knew that worship of God could have been performed just as well at home. They taught us that those whose hearts were aglow with righteousness had the Ganges in their own homes. But they saw that India was one undivided land so made by nature. They, therefore, argued that it must be one nation. Arguing thus, they established holy places in various parts of India, and fired the people with an idea of nationality in a manner unknown in other parts of the world. And we Indians are one as no two Englishmen are. Only you and I and others who consider ourselves civilized and superior persons imagine that we are many nations. It was after the advent of railways that we began to believe in distinctions, and you are at liberty now to say that it is through the railways that we are beginning to abolish those distinctions. An opium-eater may argue the advantage of opium-eating from the fact that he began to understand the evil of the opium habit after having eaten it. I would ask you to consider well what I had said on the railways.[2]

Reader : I will gladly do so, but one question occurs to me even now. You have described to me the India of the pre-Mahomedan period, but now we have Mahomedans, Parsis and Christians. How can they be one nation? Hindus and Mahomedans are old enemies.[3] Our very proverbs prove it.[4]

---

1. The original begins: "I do not say this without due reflection."
2. The original adds: "Doubts will still occur to you, but you will be able to resolve them yourself."
3. The original has: " . . . are believed to be inveterate enemies."
4. The original adds: "A Mahomedan has no use for Mahadev."

Mahomedans turn to the West for worship, whilst Hindus turn to the East. The former look down on the Hindus as idolaters.[1] The Hindus worship the cow, the Mahomedans kill her. The Hindus believe in the doctrine of non-killing, the Mahomedans do not. We thus meet with differences at every step. How can India be one nation?[2]

1. The original adds: "Hindus worship images; Mahomedans are iconoclasts."
2. The original has: "How can these disappear and India be one nation?"

10

III

The Condition of India (*Contd.*): *The Hindus and the Mahomedans*

Editor : Your last question is a serious one and yet, on careful consideration, it will be found to be easy of solution. The question arises because of the presence of the railways, of the lawyers and of the doctors. We shall presently examine the last two. We have already considered the railways. I should, however, like to add that man is so made by nature as to require him[1] to restrict his movements as far as his hands and feet will take him. If we did not rush about from place to place by means of railways and such other maddening[2] conveniences, much of the confusion that arises would be obviated. Our difficulties are of our own creation. God set a limit to man's locomotive ambition in the construction of his body. Man immediately proceeded to discover means of overriding the limit. God gifted man with intellect that he might know his Maker. Man abused it so that he might forget his Maker. I am so constructed that I can only serve my immediate neighbours, but in my conceit I pretend to have discovered that I must with my body serve every individual in the Universe. In thus attempting the impossible, man comes in contact with different natures, different religions, and[3] is utterly confounded.According to this reasoning, it must be apparent to you that railways are a most dangerous institution. Owing to them, man has gone further away from his Maker.

1. The original has: " . . . by nature that he should restrict. . . "
2. The word for "maddening" is not found in the original.
3. The original has: "and, being unable to carry the burden imposed by this, gives way to impatience."

Reader : But I am impatient to hear your answer to my question. Has the introduction of Mahomedanism not unmade the nation?

Editor : India cannot cease to be one nation because people belonging to different religions live in it. The introduction of foreigners does not necessarily destroy the nation; they merge in it. A country is one nation only when such a condition obtains in it. That country must have a faculty for assimilation. India has ever been such a country. In reality, there are as many religions as there are individuals; but those who are conscious of the spirit of nationality do not interfere with one another's religion. If they do, they are not fit to be considered a nation. If the Hindus believe that India should be peopled only by Hindus, they are living in dreamland.[1] The Hindus, the Mahomedans, the Parsis and the Christians who have made India their country are fellow countrymen, and they will have to live in unity, if only for their own interest. In no part of the world are one nationality and one religion synonymous terms; nor has it ever been so in India.

Reader : But what about the inborn enmity between Hindus and Mahomedans?

Editor : That phrase has been invented by our mutual enemy. When the Hindus and Mahomedans fought against one another, they certainly spoke in that strain. They have long since ceased to fight. How, then, can there be any inborn enmity? Pray remember this too, that we did not cease to fight only after British occupation. The Hindus flourished under Moslem sovereigns and Moslems under the Hindu. Each party recognized that mutual fighting was suicidal, and that neither party would abandon its religion by force of arms.[2] Both parties, therefore, decided to live in peace. With the English advent quarrels recommenced. The proverbs you have quoted were coined when both were fighting; to quote them now is obviously harmful. Should we not remember that many Hindus

1. The original adds: "The Mahomedans also live in dreamland if they believe that there should be only Muslims in India."
2. The original has: " . . . neither party could be made to abandon its religion or change its ways by force of arms."

and Mahomedans own the same ancestors and the same blood runs through their veins?[1] Do people become enemies because they change their religion? Is the God of the Mahomedan different from the God of the Hindu? Religions are different roads converging to the same point. What does it matter that we take different roads so long as we reach the same goal? Wherein is the cause for quarrelling?

Moreover, there are deadly proverbs as between the followers of Shiva and those of Vishnu, yet nobody suggests that these two do not belong to the same nation. It is said that the Vedic religion is different from Jainism, but the followers of the respective faiths are not different nations. The fact is that we have become enslaved and, therefore, quarrel and like to have our quarrels decided by a third party. There are Hindu iconoclasts as there are Mahomedan. The more we advance in true knowledge, the better we shall understand that we need not be at war with those whose religion we may not follow.

Reader : Now I would like to know your views about cow-protection.

Editor : I myself respect the cow, that is, I look upon her with affectionate reverence. The cow is the protector of India because, being an agricultural country, she is dependent on the cow. The cow is a most useful animal in hundreds of ways. Our Mahomedan brethren will admit this.

But, just as I respect the cow, so do I respect my fellow-men. A man is just as useful as a cow no matter whether he be a Mahomedan or a Hindu. Am I, then, to fight with or kill a Mahomedan in order to save a cow? In doing so, I would become an enemy of the Mahomedan as well as of the cow. Therefore, the only method I know of protecting the cow is that I should approach my Mahomedan brother and urge him for the sake of the country to join me in protecting her. If he would not listen to me I should let the cow go for the simple

1. The original has: "What is stated above also applies to the saying, 'A Mahomedan has no use for Mahadev.' Some sayings live on and cause mischief. Misled by the sayings, we do not even remember that many Hindus and Muslims had the same ancestors and have the same blood."

reason that the matter is beyond my ability. If I were overfull of pity for the cow, I should sacrifice my life to save her but not take my brother's. This, I hold, is the law of our religion.

When men become obstinate, it is a difficult thing. If I pull one way, my Moslem brother will pull another. If I put on superior airs, he will return the compliment. If I bow to him gently, he will do it much more so; and if he does not, I shall not be considered to have done wrong in having bowed. When the Hindus became insistent, the killing of cows increased. In my opinion, cow-protection societies may be considered cow-killing societies. It is a disgrace to us that we should need such societies. When we forgot how to protect cows, I suppose we needed such societies.

What am I to do when a blood-brother is on the point of killing a cow? Am I to kill him, or to fall down at his feet and implore him? If you admit that I should adopt the latter course, I must do the same to my Moslem brother.

Who protects the cow from destruction by Hindus when they cruelly ill-treat her? Whoever reasons with the Hindus when they mercilessly belabour the progeny of the cow with their sticks? But this has not prevented us from remaining one nation.

Lastly, if it be true that the Hindus believe in the doctrine of non-killing and the Mahomedans do not, what, pray, is the duty of the former? It is not written that a follower of the religion of *ahimsa* (nonkilling) may kill a fellow-man. For him the way is straight. In order to save one being, he may not kill another. He can only plead—therein lies his sole duty.

But does every Hindu believe in *ahimsa*? Going to the root of the matter, not one man really practises such a religion because we do destroy life. We are said to follow that religion because we want to obtain freedom from liability to kill any kind of life. Generally speaking, we may observe that many Hindus partake of meat and are not, therefore, followers of *ahimsa*.[1] It is, therefore, preposterous to suggest that the two

1. The original adds: "I have nothing to say if anyone is bent upon stretching the meanings of words so as to prove his point."

cannot live together amicably because the Hindus believe in *ahimsa* and the Mahomedans do not.

These thoughts are put into our minds by selfish and false religious teachers. The English put the finishing touch. They have a habit of writing history; they pretend to study the manners and customs of all peoples. God has given us a limited mental capacity, but they usurp the function of the Godhead and indulge in novel experiments. They write about their own researches in most laudatory terms and hypnotize us into believing them. We in our ignorance then fall at their feet.[1]

Those who do not wish to misunderstand things may read up the *Koran,* and they will find therein hundreds of passages acceptable to the Hindus; and the *Bhagavad Gita* contains passages to which not a Mahomedan can take exception. Am I to dislike a Mahomedan because there are passages in the *Koran* I do not understand or like? It takes two to make a quarrel. If I do not want to quarrel with a Mahomedan, the latter will be powerless to foist a quarrel on me; and, similarly, I should be powerless if a Mahomedan refuses his assistance to quarrel with me. An arm striking the air will become disjointed. If everyone will try to understand the core of his own religion and adhere to it, and will not allow false teachers to dictate to him, there will be no room left for quarrelling.

Reader : But will the English ever allow the two bodies to join hands?

Editor : This question arises out of your timidity. It betrays our shallowness. If two brothers want to live in peace, is it possible for a third party to separate them? If they were to listen to evil counsels we would consider them to be foolish. Similarly, we Hindus and Mahomedans would have to blame our folly rather than the English, if we allowed them to put us asunder. A clay pot would break through impact, if not with one stone, then with another. The way to save the pot is not to keep it away from the danger point but to bake it so that no stone would break it. We have then to make our hearts of perfectly baked clay. Then we shall be steeled against all

1. The original has: "We in our simplicity believe all that they say".

danger.[1] This can be easily done by the Hindus.[2] They are superior in numbers; they pretend that they are more educated; they are, therefore, better able to shield themselves from attack on their amicable relations with the Mahomedans.[3]

There is mutual distrust between the two communities. The Mahomedans, therefore, ask for certain concessions from Lord Morley. Why should the Hindus oppose this? If the Hindus desisted, the English would notice it, the Mahomedans would gradually begin to trust the Hindus, and brotherliness would be the outcome. We should be ashamed to take our quarrels to the English. Everyone can find out for himself that the Hindus can lose nothing by desisting. That man who has inspired confidence in another has never lost anything in this world.

I do not suggest that the Hindus and the Mahomedans will never fight. Two brothers living together often do so. We shall sometimes have our heads broken. Such a thing ought not to be necessary, but all men are not equitable.[4] When people are in a rage, they do many foolish things. These we have to put up with. But when we do quarrel, we certainly do not want to engage counsel and resort to English or any law-courts. Two men fight; both have their heads broken, or one only. How shall a third party distribute justice amongst them? Those who fight may expect to be injured.[5]

---

1. The original has: "Should even one side be sound of heart, the third party will not succeed in its designs."
2. The original has: "The Hindus can easily afford to be so."
3. The original has: "; it should, therefore, be possible for them to have a heart of well-baked clay".
4. The original has: "equally sensible".
5. The original adds: "When human bodies clash against one another, some marks are bound to be left on them. Where is the question of awarding justice in this matter?"

11

IV

The Condition of India (*Contd.*): *Lawyers*

Reader : You tell me that when two men quarrel they should not go to a law-court. This is astonishing.

Editor : Whether you call it astonishing or not, it is the truth. And your question introduces us to the lawyers and the doctors. My firm[1] opinion is that the lawyers have enslaved India, have accentuated Hindu-Mahomedan dissensions and have confirmed English authority.

Reader : It is easy enough to bring these charges, but it will be difficult for you to prove them. But for the lawyers, who would have shown us the road to independence? Who would have protected the poor? Who would have secured justice? For instance, the late Manomohan Ghose[2] defended many a poor man free of charge. The Congress, which you have praised so much, is dependent for its existence and activity upon the work of the lawyers. To denounce such an estimable[3] class of men is to spell injustice,[4] and you are abusing the liberty of the Press by decrying lawyers.

Editor : At one time I used to think exactly like you. I have no desire to convince you that they have never done a single good thing. I honour Mr. Ghose's memory. It is quite true that he helped the poor. That the Congress owes the

1. The word "firm" is not found in the original.
2. (1844-96), lawyer and Congressman; first Indian barrister; founder and editor of *Indian Mirror.*
3. The word for "estimable" is not found in the original.
4. The original has: "is to treat justice as injustice".

lawyers something is believable. Lawyers are also men, and there is something good in every man. Whenever instances of lawyers having done good can be brought forward, it will be found that the good is due to them as men rather than as lawyers. All I am concerned with is to show you that the profession teaches immorality; it is exposed to temptation from which few are saved.

The Hindus and the Mahomedans have quarrelled. An ordinary man will ask them to forget all about it; he will tell them that both must be more or less at fault, and will advise them no longer to quarrel. But they go to lawyers. The latter's duty is to side with their clients and to find out ways and arguments in favour of the clients, to which they (the clients) are often strangers. If they do not do so, they will be considered to have degraded their profession. The lawyers, therefore, will, as a rule, advance quarrels instead of repressing them.[1] Moreover, men take up that profession, not in order to help others out of their miseries, but to enrich themselves. It is one of the avenues of becoming wealthy and their interest exists in multiplying disputes. It is within my knowledge that they are glad when men have disputes. Petty pleaders actually manufacture them. Their touts, like so many leeches, suck the blood of the poor people.[2] Lawyers are men who have little to do. Lazy people, in order to indulge in luxuries, take up such professions. This is a true statement. Any other argument is a mere pretension. It is the lawyers who have discovered that theirs is an honourable profession. They frame laws as they frame their own praises. They decide what fees they will charge and they put on so much side that poor people almost consider them to be heaven-born.

Why do they want more fees than common labourers? Why are their requirements greater? In what way are they more profitable to the country than the labourers? Are those who do good entitled to greater payment? And, if they have done

1. The original has: "As a rule, therefore, the lawyer will be for taking further action in the dispute."
2. The original adds: "It is a profession which cannot but result in encouragement of quarrels."

anything for the country for the sake of money, how shall it be counted as good?[1]

Those who know anything of the Hindu-Mahomedan quarrels know that they have been often due to the intervention or lawyers. Some families have been ruined through them; they have made brothers enemies. Principalities, having come under the lawyers' power, have become loaded with debt. Many have been robbed of their all.[2] Such instances can be multiplied.

But the greatest injury they have done to the country is that they have tightened the English grip. Do you think that it would be possible for the English to carry on their Government without law courts? It is wrong to consider that courts are established for the benefit of the people. Those who want to perpetuate their power do so through the courts. If people were to settle their own quarrels, a third party would not be able to exercise any authority over them. Truly, men were less unmanly when they settled their disputes either by fighting or by asking their relatives to decide for them. They became more unmanly and cowardly when they resorted to the courts of law. It was certainly a sign of savagery when they settled their disputes by fighting. Is it any the less so, if I ask a third party to decide between you and me? Surely, the decision of a third party is not always right. The parties alone know who is right. We, in our simplicity and ignorance, imagine that a stranger, by taking our money, gives us justice.

The chief thing, however, to be remembered is that without lawyers courts could not have been established or conducted and without the latter the English could not rule. Supposing that there were only English judges, English pleaders and English police, they could only rule over the English. The English could not do without Indian judges and Indian pleaders. How the pleaders were made in the first

1. The original adds: "What I have pointed out is the inherent tendency of the profession itself. That was, however, by the way."
2. The original has: "Many a land owner with hereditary title in State lands has found himself robbed of his all through lawyers' machinations."

instance and how they were favoured[1] you should understand well. Then you will have the same abhorrence for the profession that I have.[2] If pleaders were to abandon their profession, and consider it just as degrading as prostitution, English rule would break up in a day. They have been instrumental in having the charge laid against us that we love quarrels and courts as fish love water. What I have said with reference to the pleaders necessarily applies to the judges; they are first cousins; and the one gives strength to the other.

1. The original has: "and how they struggled for favours. . ."
2. The original adds: "Among the chief features of British rule which account for its success are the courts, and these depend upon lawyers."

12

V
The Condition of India (*Contd.*): *Doctors*

Reader : I now understand the lawyers; the good they may have done is accidental. I feel that profession is certainly hateful. You, however, drag in the doctors also, how is that?

Editor : The views I submit to you are those I have adopted. They are not original. Western writers have used stronger terms regarding both lawyers and doctors. One writer has likened the whole modern system to the *Upas* tree. Its branches are represented by parasitical professions, including those of law and medicine, and over the trunk has been raised the axe of true religion. Immorality is the root of the tree. So you will see that the views do not come right out of my mind but represent the combined experiences of many. I was at one time a great lover of the medical profession. It was my intention to become a doctor for the sake of the country. I no longer hold that opinion. I now understand why the medicine men (the *vaids*) among us have not occupied a very honourable status.

The English have certainly effectively used the medical profession for holding us. English physicians are known to have used their profession with several Asiatic potentates for political gain.[1]

1. Instead of the last sentence, the original has: "The pretensions of physicians also know no bounds. It was a British physician who played upon the credulity of the Moghul Emperor. He was successful in treating an illness in the Emperor's family and was in consequence rewarded. It was again a physician who ingratiated himself with the Ameer."

Doctors have almost unhinged us. Sometimes I think that quacks are better than highly qualified doctors. Let us consider: the business of a doctor is to take care of the body, or, properly speaking, not even that. Their business is really to rid the body of diseases that may afflict it. How do these diseases arise? Surely by our negligence or indulgence. I overeat, I have indigestion, I go to a doctor, he gives me medicine, I am cured. I overeat again, I take his pills again. Had I not taken the pills in the first instance, I would have suffered the punishment deserved by me and I would not have overeaten again. The doctor intervened and helped me to indulge myself. My body thereby certainly felt more at ease; but my mind became weakened. A continuance of a course of medicine must, therefore, result in loss of control over the mind.

I have indulged in vice, I contract a disease, a doctor cures me, the odds are that I shall repeat the vice. Had the doctor not intervened, nature would have done its work, and I would have acquired mastery over myself, would have been freed from vice and would have become happy.

Hospitals are institutions for propagating sin. Men take less care of their bodies and immorality increases. European doctors are the worst of all. For the sake of a mistaken care of the human body, they kill annually thousands of animals. They practise vivisection. No religion sanctions this. All say that it is not necessary to take so many lives for the sake of our bodies.

These doctors violate our religious instinct. Most of their medical preparations contain either animal fat or spirituous liquors; both of these are tabooed by Hindus and Mahomedans. We may pretend to be civilized, call religious prohibitions a superstition and want only to indulge in what we like. The fact remains that the doctors induce us to indulge, and the result is that we have become deprived of self-control and have become effeminate. In these circumstances, we are unfit to serve the country. To study European medicine is to deepen our slavery.

It is worth considering why we take up the profession of medicine. It is certainly not taken up for the purpose of serving humanity. We become doctors so that we may obtain honours and riches. I have endeavoured to show that there is no real service of humanity in the profession, and that it is injurious to mankind. Doctors make a show of their knowledge, and charge exorbitant fees. Their preparations, which are intrinsically worth a few pence, cost shillings. The populace, in its credulity and in the hope of ridding itself of some disease, allows itself to be cheated. Are not quacks then, whom we know, better than the doctors who put on an air of humaneness?

13

What is True Civilization ?

Reader : You have denounced railways, lawyers and doctors. I can see that you will discard all machinery. What, then, is civilization?

Editor : The answer to that question is not difficult. I believe that the civilization India has evolved is not to be beaten in the world. Nothing can equal the seeds sown by our ancestors. Rome went, Greece shared the same fate; the might of the Pharaohs was broken; Japan has become westernized; of China nothing can be said; but India is still, somehow or other, sound at the foundation. The people of Europe learn their lessons from the writings of the men of Greece or Rome, which exist no longer in their former glory. In trying to learn from them, the Europeans imagine that they will avoid the mistakes of Greece and Rome. Such is their pitiable condition. In the midst of all this India remains immovable and that is her glory. It is a charge against India that her people are so uncivilized, ignorant and stolid, that it is not possible to induce them to adopt any changes. It is a charge really against our merit. What we have tested and found true on the anvil of experience, we dare not change. Many thrust their advice upon India, and she remains steady. This is her beauty: it is the sheet-anchor of our hope.

Civilization is that mode of conduct which points out to man the path of duty. Performance of duty and observance of morality are convertible terms. To observe morality is to attain mastery over our mind and our passions. So doing, we know ourselves. The Gujarati equivalent for civilization means "good conduct".[1]

If this definition be correct, then India, as so many writers[2] have shown,[3] has nothing to learn from anybody else, and this is as it should be. We notice that the mind is a restless bird; the more it gets the more it wants, and still remains unsatisfied. The more we indulge our passions, the more unbridled they become. Our ancestors, therefore, set a limit to our indulgences. They saw that happiness was largely a mental condition. A man is not necessarily happy because he is rich, or unhappy because he is poor. The rich are often seen to be unhappy, the poor to be happy. Millions will always remain poor. Observing all this, our ancestors dissuaded us from luxuries and pleasures. We have managed with the same kind of plough as existed thousands of years ago. We have retained the same kind of cottages that we had in former times and our indigenous education remains the same as before. We have had no system of life-corroding competition. Each followed his own occupation or trade and charged a regulation wage. It was not that we did not know how to invent machinery, but our forefathers knew that, if we set our hearts after such things, we would become slaves and lose our moral fibre. They, therefore, after due deliberation decided that we should only do what we could with our hands and feet. They saw that our real happiness and health consisted in a proper use of our hands and feet.

They further reasoned that large cities were a snare and a useless encumbrance and that people would not be happy in them, that there would be gangs of thieves and robbers, prostitution and vice flourishing in them and that poor men would be robbed by rich men. They were, therefore, satisfied with small villages. They saw that kings and their swords were inferior to the sword of ethics, and they, therefore, held the

1. Literally, "This is the meaning of *su*, that is, good, *dharo* [way of life]." The original adds: "The opposite is *Kudharo* [bad way of life]."
2. The original has "British writers".
3. *Vide* "Testimonies by Eminent Men", Appendix II to *Hind Swaraj*, 5-12-1820.

sovereigns of the earth to be inferior to the *rishis*[1] and the *fakirs*[2]. A nation with a constitution like this is fitter to teach others than to learn from others. This nation had courts, lawyers and doctors, but they were all within bounds. Everybody knew that these professions were not particularly superior; moreover, these *vakils*[3] and *vaids*[4] did not rob people; they were considered people's dependants, not their masters. Justice was tolerably fair. The ordinary rule was to avoid courts. There were no touts to lure people into them. This evil, too, was noticeable only in and around capitals. The common people lived independently and followed their agricultural occupation. They enjoyed true Home Rule.

And where this cursed modern civilization has not reached, India remains as it was before. The inhabitants of that part of India will very properly laugh at your new-fangled notions. The English do not rule over them, nor will you ever rule over them. Those in whose name we speak we do not know, nor do they know us. I would certainly advise you and those like you who love the motherland to go into the interior that has yet been not polluted by the railways and to live there for six months; you might then be patriotic and speak of Home Rule.

Now you see what I consider to be real civilization. Those who want to change conditions such as I have described are enemies of the country and are sinners.

Reader : It would be all right if India were exactly as you have described it, but it is also India where there are hundreds of child widows, where two-year old babies are married, where twelve-year old girls are mothers and housewives, where women practise polyandry, where the practice of *niyoga*[5] obtains, where, in the name of religion, girls dedicate themselves to prostitution, and in the name of religion sheep[6] and goats are killed. Do you consider these also symbols of the civilization that you have described?

1. Sages
2. Ascetics.
3. Lawyers
4. Doctors .
5. Insemination by a person other than one's husband.
6. The original has: "he-buffaloes".

Editor : You make a mistake. The defects that you have shown are defects. Nobody mistakes them for ancient civilization. They remain in spite of it. Attempts have always been made and will be made to remove them. We may utilize the new spirit that is born in us for purging ourselves of these evils. But what I have described to you as emblems of modern civilization are accepted as such by its votaries. The Indian civilization, as described by me, has been so described by its votaries. In no part of the world, and under no civilization, have all men attained perfection. The tendency of the Indian civilization is to elevate the moral being, that of the Western civilization is to propagate immorality. The latter is godless, the former is based on a belief in God. So understanding and so believing, it behoves every lover of India to cling to the old Indian civilization even as a child clings to the mother's breast.

14

How can India become Free?

Reader : I appreciate your views about civilization. I will have to think over them. I cannot take them in all at once. What, then, holding the views you do, would you suggest for freeing India?

Editor : I do not expect my views to be accepted all of a sudden. My duty is to place them before readers like yourself. Time can be trusted to do the rest[1].We have already examined the conditions for freeing India, but we have done so indirectly; we will now do so directly. It is a world-known maxim that the removal of the cause of a disease results in the removal of the disease itself. Similarly, if the cause of India's slavery be removed, India can become free.

Reader : If Indian civilization is, as you say, the best of all, how do you account for India's slavery?

Editor : This civilization is unquestionably the best, but it is to be observed that all civilizations have been on their trial. That civilization which is permanent outlives it. Because the sons of India were found wanting, its civilization has been placed in jeopardy. But its strength is to be seen in its ability to survive the shock. Moreover, the whole of India is not touched. Those alone who have been affected by Western civilization have become enslaved. We measure the universe by our own miserable foot-rule. When we are slaves, we think that the whole universe is enslaved. Because we are in an abject condition, we think that the whole of India is in that condition.

---

1. The original has: "Time will show whether they find them acceptable or not."

As a matter of fact, it is not so, yet it is as well to impute our slavery to the whole of India. But if we bear in mind the above fact, we can see that if we become free, India is free. And in this thought you have a definition of *Swaraj*. It is *Swaraj* when we learn to rule ourselves. It is, therefore, in the palm of our hands. Do not consider this *Swaraj* to be like a dream. There is no idea of sitting still. The *Swaraj* that I wish to picture is such that, after we have once realized it, we shall endeavour to the end of our life-time to persuade others to do likewise. But such *Swaraj* has to be experienced, by each one for himself. One drowning man will never save another. Slaves ourselves, it would be a mere pretension to think of freeing others. Now you will have seen that it is not necessary for us to have as our goal the expulsion of the English. If the English become Indianized, we can accommodate them. If they wish to remain in India along with their civilization, there is no room for them. It lies with us to bring about such a state of things.

Reader : It is impossible that Englishmen should ever become Indianized.

Editor : To say that is equivalent to saying that the English have no humanity in them. And it is really besides the point whether they become so or not. If we keep our own house in order, only those who are fit to live in it will remain. Others will leave of their own accord. Such things occur within the experience of all of us.

Reader : But it has not occurred in history.

Editor : To believe that what has not occurred in history will not occur at all is to argue disbelief in the dignity of man. At any rate, it behoves us to try what appeals to our reason. All countries are not similarly conditioned. The condition of India is unique. Its strength is immeasurable. We need not, therefore, refer to the history of other countries. I have drawn attention to the fact that, when other civilizations have succumbed, the Indian has survived many a shock.

Reader : I cannot follow this. There seems little doubt that we shall have to expel the English by force of arms. So long as they are in the country we cannot rest. One of our poets says that slaves cannot even dream of happiness. We are day by day becoming weakened owing to the presence of the English. Our greatness is gone; our people look like terrified men. The English are in the country like a blight which we must remove by every means.

Editor : In your excitement, you have forgotten all we have been considering. We brought the English, and we keep them. Why do you forget that our adoption of their civilization makes their presence in India at all possible? Your hatred against them ought to be transferred to their civilization. But let us assume that we have to drive away the English by fighting, how is that to be done?

Reader : In the same way as Italy did it. What was possible for Mazzini[1] and Garibaldi[2] is possible for us. You cannot deny that they were very great men.

1. Giuseppe Mazzini (1805-72); *vide* "Joseph Mazzini", 22-7-1905.
2. Giuseppe Garibaldi (1807-82), Italian soldier and patriot, one of the leaders in the struggle for unification of Italy; *vide* Vol. V, p. 28.

15

Italy and India

Editor : It is well that you have instanced Italy. Mazzini was a great and good man; Garibaldi was a great warrior. Both are adorable; from their lives we can learn much. But the condition of Italy was different from that of India. In the first instance, the difference between Mazzini and Garibaldi is worth noting. Mazzini's ambition was not and has not yet been realized regarding Italy. Mazzini has shown in his writings on the duty of man that every man must learn how to rule himself. This has not happened in Italy. Garibaldi did not hold this view of Mazzini. Garibaldi gave and every Italian took arms. Italy and Austria had the same civilization; they were cousins in this respect. It was a matter of tit for tat. Garibaldi simply wanted Italy to be free from the Austrian yoke. The machinations of Minister Cavour[1] disgrace that portion of the history of Italy. And what has been the result? If you believe that because Italians rule Italy the Italian nation is happy, you are groping in darkness. Mazzini has shown conclusively that Italy did not become free. Victor Emmanuel [II] gave one meaning to the expression; Mazzini gave another. According to Emmanuel, Cavour and even Garibaldi, Italy meant the King of Italy and his henchmen. According to Mazzini, it meant the whole of the Italian people, that is, its agriculturists. Emmanuel was only its servant. The Italy of Mazzini still remains in a state of

1. Count Camillo Benso Cavour (1810-61), distinguished Italian statesman, who, as Premier to Victor Emmanuel, King of Sardinia (proclaimed King of Italy in 1861), did much for the unification of Italy which was achieved in 1870.

slavery. At the time of the so-called national war, it was a game of chess between two rival kings with the people of Italy as pawns. The working classes in that land are still unhappy. They, therefore, indulge in assassination, rise in revolt, and rebellion on their part is always expected. What substantial gain did Italy obtain after the withdrawal of the Austrian troops? The gain was only nominal. The reforms for the sake of which the war was supposed to have been undertaken have not yet been granted. The condition of the people in general still remains the same. I am sure you do not wish to reproduce such a condition in India. I believe that you want the millions of India to be happy, not that you want the reins of government in your hands. If that be so, we have to consider only one thing: how can the millions obtain self-rule? You will admit that people under several Indian princes are being ground down. The latter mercilessly crush them. Their tyranny is greater than that of the English, and if you want such tyranny in India, then we shall never agree. My patriotism does not teach me that I am to allow people to be crushed under the heel of Indian princes if only the English retire. If I have the power, I should resist the tyranny of Indian princes just as much as that of the English. By patriotism I mean the welfare of the whole people, and if I could secure it at the hands of the English, I should bow down my head to them. If any Englishman dedicated his life to securing the freedom of India, resisting tyranny and serving the land, I should welcome that Englishman as an Indian.

Again, India can fight like Italy only when she has arms. You have not considered this problem at all. The English are splendidly armed; that does not frighten me, but it is clear that, to pit ourselves against them in arms, thousands of Indians must be armed. If such a thing be possible, how many years will it take? Moreover, to arm India on a large scale is to Europeanize it. Then her condition will be just as pitiable as that of Europe. This means, in short, that India must accept European civilization, and if that is what we want, the best thing is that we have among us those who are so well trained in that civilization. We will then fight for a few rights, will get what we can and so pass our days. But the fact is that the Indian nation will not adopt arms, and it is well that it does not.

Reader : You are overstating the facts. All need not be armed. At first, we shall assassinate a few Englishmen and strike terror; then, a few men who will have been armed will fight openly. We may have to lose a quarter[1] of a million men, more or less, but we shall regain our land. We shall undertake guerrilla warfare, and defeat the English.

Editor : That is to say, you want to make the holy land of India unholy. Do you not tremble to think of freeing India by assassination? What we need to do is to sacrifice ourselves. It is a cowardly thought, that of killing others. Whom do you suppose to free by assassination? The millions of India do not desire it. Those who are intoxicated by the wretched modern civilization think these things. Those who will rise to power by murder will certainly not make the nation happy. Those who believe that India has gained by Dhingra's act[2] and other similar acts[3] in India make a serious mistake. Dhingra was a patriot, but his love was blind. He gave his body in a wrong way; its ultimate result can only be mischievous.

Reader : But you will admit that the English have been frightened by these murders, and that Lord Morley's[4] reforms are due to fear.

Editor : The English are both a timid and a brave nation. England is, I believe, easily influenced by the use of gunpowder. It is possible that Lord Morley has granted the reforms through fear, but what is granted under fear can be retained only so long as the fear lasts.

---

1. The original has: "2,000,000 or 2,500,000 men".
2. *Vide footnote 1, p.4*
3. *Vide footnote 2, p.14.*
4. Morley was Secretary of State for India. The Morley-Minto Reforms came into force on November 15, 1909.

16

Brute Force

Reader : This is a new doctrine, that what is gained through fear is retained only while the fear lasts. Surely, what is given will not be withdrawn?

Editor : Not so. The Proclamation of 1857[1] was given at the end of a revolt, and for the purpose of preserving peace. When peace was secured and people became simple-minded, its full effect was toned down. If I cease stealing for fear of punishment, I would recommence the operation as soon as the fear is withdrawn from me. This is almost a universal experience. We have assumed that we can get men to do things by force and, therefore, we use force.

Reader : Will you not admit that you are arguing against yourself? You know that what the English obtained in their own country they obtained by using brute force. I know you have argued that what they have obtained is useless, but that does not affect my argument. They wanted useless things and they got them. My point is that their desire was fulfilled. What does it matter what means they adopted? Why should we not obtain our goal, which is good, by any means whatsoever, even by using violence? Shall I think of the means when I have to deal with a thief in the house? My duty is to drive him out anyhow. You seem to admit that we have received nothing, and that we shall receive nothing, by petitioning. Why, then, may we not do so by using brute force? And, to retain what we may receive, we shall keep up the fear by using the same force to the extent that it may be necessary. You will not find

1. Queen Victoria's Proclamation of 1858.

fault with a continuance of force to prevent a child from thrusting its foot into fire? Somehow or other we have to gain our end.

Editor : Your reasoning is plausible. It has deluded many. I have used similar arguments before now. But I think I know better now, and I shall endeavour to undeceive you. Let us first take the argument that we are justified in gaining our end by using brute force because the English gained theirs by using similar means. It is perfectly true that they used brute force and that it is possible for us to do likewise, but by using similar means we can get only the same thing that they got. You will admit that we do not want that. Your belief that there is no connection between the means and the end is a great mistake. Through that mistake even men who have been considered religious have committed grievous crimes. Your reasoning is the same as saying that we can get a rose through planting a noxious weed. If I want to cross the ocean, I can do so only by means of a vessel; if I were to use a cart for that purpose, both the cart and I would soon find the bottom. "As is the God, so is the votary", is a maxim worth considering. Its meaning has been distorted and men have gone astray. The means may be likened to a seed, the end to a tree; and there is just the same inviolable connection between the means and the end as there is between the seed and the tree. I am not likely to obtain the result flowing from the worship of God by laying myself prostrate before Satan. If, therefore, anyone were to say: "I want to worship God; it does not matter that I do so by means of Satan", it would be set down as ignorant folly. We reap exactly as we sow. The English in 1833 obtained greater voting power by violence. Did they by using brute force better appreciate their duty ? They wanted the right of voting, which they obtained by using physical force. But real rights are a result of performance of duty; these rights they have not obtained. We, therefore, have before us in England the force[1] of everybody

1. Probably a misprint for "farce". The original has: "The result has been that everyone is found to be running after rights, giving no thought to duties."

wanting and insisting on his rights, nobody thinking of his duty. And, where everybody wants rights, who shall give them to whom? I do not wish to imply that they do no duties. They don't perform the duties corresponding to those rights; and as they do not perform that particular duty, namely, acquire fitness, their rights have proved a burden to them. In other words, what they have obtained is an exact result of the means they adopted. They used the means corresponding to the end. If I want to deprive you of your watch, I shall certainly have to fight for it; if I want to buy your watch, I shall have to pay you for it; and if I want a gift I shall have to plead for it; and, according to the means I employ, the watch is stolen property, my own property, or a donation. Thus we see three different results from three different means. Will you still say that means do not matter?

Now we shall take the example given by you of the thief to be driven out. I do not agree with you that the thief may be driven out by any means. If it is my father who has come to steal I shall use one kind of means. If it is an acquaintance I shall use another; and in the case of a perfect stranger I shall use a third. If it is a white man, you will perhaps say you will use means different from those you will adopt with an Indian thief. If it is a weakling, the means will be different from those to be adopted for dealing with an equal in physical strength; and if the thief is armed from top to toe, I shall simply remain quiet. Thus we have a variety of means between the father and the armed man. Again, I fancy that I should pretend to be sleeping whether the thief was my father or that strong armed man. The reason for this is that my father would also be armed and I should succumb to the strength possessed by either and allow my things to be stolen. The strength of my father would make me weep with pity; the strength of the armed man would rouse in me anger and we should become enemies. Such is the curious situation. From these examples we may not be able to agree as to the means to be adopted in each case. I myself seem clearly to see what should be done in all these cases, but the remedy may frighten you. I, therefore, hesitate to place it before you. For the time being I will leave you to guess it, and if you cannot, it is clear you will have to adopt different means in each case. You will also have seen that any means will not avail to drive away the thief. You will have to adopt means to fit each case. Hence it follows that your duty is *not* to drive away the thief by any means you like.

Let us proceed a little further. That well-armed man has stolen your property; you have harboured the thought of his act; you are filled with anger; you argue that you want to punish that rogue, not for your own sake, but for the good of your neighbours; you have collected a number of armed men, you want to take his house by assault; he is duly informed of it, he runs away; he too is incensed. He collects his brother-robbers, and sends you a defiant message that he will commit robbery in broad daylight. You are strong, you do not fear him, you are prepared to receive him. Meanwhile, the robber pesters your neighbours. They complain before you. You reply that you are doing all for their sake, you do not mind that your own goods have been stolen. Your neighbours reply that the robber never pestered them before, and that he commenced his depredations only after you declared hostilities against him. You are between Scylla and Charybdis. You are full of pity for the poor men. What they say is true. What are you to do? You will be disgraced if you now leave the robber alone. You, therefore, tell the poor men: "Never mind. Come, my wealth is yours, I will give you arms, I will teach you how to use them; you should be labour the rogue; don't you leave him alone." And so the battle grows; the robbers increase in numbers; your neighbours have deliberately put themselves to inconvenience. Thus the result of wanting to take revenge upon the robber is that you have disturbed your own peace; you are in perpetual fear of being robbed and assaulted; your courage has given place to cowardice. If you will patiently examine the argument, you will see that I have not overdrawn the picture. This is one of the means. Now let us examine the other. You set this armed robber down as an ignorant brother; you intend to reason with him at a suitable opportunity: you argue that he is, after all, a fellow man; you do not know what prompted him to steal. You, therefore, decide that, when you can, you will destroy the man's motive for stealing. Whilst you are thus reasoning with yourself the man comes again to steal. Instead of being angry with him, you take pity on him. You think that this stealing habit must be a disease with him. Henceforth, you, therefore, keep your doors and windows open, you change your sleeping place, and you keep your things in a manner most accessible to him. The robber comes again and is confused as all this is new to him; nevertheless, he takes away your things. But his mind is agitated. He inquires about you in the village, he comes to learn about your broad and loving heart, he repents, he begs your pardon, returns you your things, and leaves off the stealing habit. He becomes your servant, and you find for him honourable employment. This is the second method. Thus, you see, different means have brought about totally different results. I do not wish to deduce from this that robbers will act in the above manner or that all will have the same pity and love like you, but I only wish to show that fair means alone can produce fair results, and that, at least in the majority of cases, if not indeed in all, the force of love and pity is infinitely greater than the force of arms. There is harm in the exercise of brute force, never in that of pity.

Now we will take the question of petitioning. It is a fact beyond dispute that a petition, without the backing of force, is useless. However, the late Justice Ranade[1] used to say that petitions served a useful purpose because they were a means of educating people. They give the latter an idea of their condition and warn the rulers. From this point of view, they are not altogether useless. A petition of an equal is a sign of courtesy; a petition from a slave is a symbol of his slavery. A petition backed by force is a petition from an equal and, when he transmits his demand in the form of a petition, it testifies to his nobility. Two kinds of force can back petitions. "We shall hurt you if you do not give this," is one kind of force; it is the force of arms, whose evil results we have already examined. The second kind of force can thus be stated: "If you do not concede our demand, we shall be no longer your petitioners. You can govern us only so long as we remain the governed; we shall no longer have any dealings with you." The force

1. Mahadev Govind Ranade (1842-1901), distinguished Indian judge, social reformer, author and one of the founders of the Indian National Congress.

implied in this may be described as love-force, soul-force, or, more popularly but less accurately, passive resistance.[1]

This force is indestructible. He who uses it perfectly understands his position. We have an ancient proverb which literally means: "One negative cures thirty-six diseases." The force of arms is powerless when matched against the force of love or the soul. Now we shall take your last illustration, that of the child thrusting its foot into fire. It will not avail you. What do you really do to the child ? Supposing that it can exert so much physical force that it renders you powerless and rushes into fire, then you cannot prevent it. There are only two remedies open to you—either you must kill it in order to prevent it from perishing in the flames, or you must give your own life because you do not wish to see it perish before your very eyes. You will not kill it. If your heart is not quite full of pity, it is possible that you will not surrender yourself by preceding the child and going into the fire yourself. You, therefore, helplessly allow it to go into the flames. Thus, at any rate, you are not using physical force. I hope you will not consider that it is still physical force, though of a low order, when you would forcibly prevent the child from rushing towards the fire if you could. That force is of a different order and we have to understand what it is. Remember that, in thus preventing the child, you are minding entirely its own interest, you are exercising authority for its sole benefit. Your example does not apply to the English. In using brute force against the English you consult entirely your own, that is the national interest. There is no question here either of pity or of love. If you say that the actions of the English, being evil, represent fire, and that they proceed to their actions through ignorance, and that therefore they occupy the position of a child and that you want to protect such a child, then you will have to overtake every evil action of that kind by whomsoever committed and, as in the case of the evil child, you will have to sacrifice yourself. If you are capable of such immeasurable pity, I wish you well in its exercise.[2]

---

1. Instead of "more popularly but less accurately, passive resistance", the original has the one word "satyagraha".
2. The original adds: "The thing is simply impossible."

17

Passive Resistance[1]

Reader : Is there any historical evidence as to the success of what you have called soul-force or truth-force? No instance seems to have happened of any nation having risen through soul-force. I still think that the evil-doers will not cease doing evil without physical punishment.

Editor : The poet Tulsidas has said: "Of religion, pity, or love, is the root, as egotism of the body. Therefore, we should not abandon pity so long as we are alive." This appears to me to be a scientific truth. I believe in it as much as I believe in two and two being four. The force of love is the same as the force of the soul or truth. We have evidence of its working at every step. The universe would disappear without the existence of that force. But you ask for historical evidence. It is, therefore, necessary to know what history means. The Gujarati equivalent means: "It so happened."[2] If that is the meaning of history, it is possible to give copious evidence. But, if it means the doings of kings and emperors, there can be no evidence of soul-force or passive resistance in such history. You cannot expect silver ore in a tin mine. History, as we know it, is a record of the wars of the world, and so there is a proverb among Englishmen that a nation which has no history, that is, no wars, is a happy nation. How kings played, how they became enemies of one another, how they murdered one another, is found accurately recorded in history, and if this were all that had happened in the world, it would have been ended long ago. If the story of

1. The original has: "Satyagraha—Soul-force".
2. Literally, "*Itihas* [history] means 'it so happened'."

the universe had commenced with wars, not a man would have been found alive today. Those people who have been warred against have disappeared as, for instance, the natives of Australia of whom hardly a man was left alive by the intruders. Mark, please, that these natives did not use soul-force in self-defence, and it does not require much foresight to know that the Australians will share the same fate as their victims. "Those that take the sword shall perish by the sword." With us the proverb is that professional swimmers will find a watery grave.

The fact that there are so many men still alive in the world shows that it is based not on the force of arms but on the force of truth or love. Therefore, the greatest and most unimpeachable evidence of the success of this force is to be found in the fact that, in spite of the wars of the world, it still lives on.

Thousands, indeed tens of thousands, depend for their existence on a very active working of this force. Little quarrels of millions of families in their daily lives disappear before the exercise of this force.Hundreds of nations live in peace. History does not and cannot take note of this fact. History is really a record of every interruption of the even working of the force of love or of the soul. Two brothers quarrel; one of them repents and re-awakens the love that was lying dormant in him;[1] the two again begin to live in peace; nobody takes note of this. But if the two brothers, through the intervention of solicitors or some other reason take up arms or go to law—which is another form of the exhibition of brute force,—their doings would be immediately noticed in the Press, they would be the talk of their neighbours and would probably go down to history. And what is true of families and communities is true of nations. There is no reason to believe that there is one law for families and another for nations. History, then, is a record of an interruption of the course of nature. Soul-force, being natural, is not noted in history.

Reader : According to what you say, it is plain that instances of this kind of passive resistance are not to be found

1. The original has: "one of them practises satyagraha against the other".

in history. It is necessary to understand this passive resistance more fully. It will be better, therefore, if you enlarge upon it.

Editor : Passive resistance is a method of securing rights by personal suffering; it is the reverse of resistance by arms.[1] When I refuse to do a thing that is repugnant to my conscience, I use soul-force. For instance, the Government of the day has passed a law which is applicable to me. I do not like it. If by using violence I force the Government to repeal the law, I am employing what may be termed body-force. If I do not obey the law and accept the penalty for its breach, I use soul-force. It involves sacrifice of self.

Everybody admits that sacrifice of self is infinitely superior to sacrifice of others. Moreover, if this kind of force is used in a cause that is unjust, only the person using it suffers. He does not make others suffer for his mistakes. Men have before now done many things which were subsequently found to have been wrong. No man can claim that he is absolutely in the right or that a particular thing is wrong because he thinks so, but it is wrong for him so long as that is his deliberate judgment. It is, therefore, meet that he should not do that which he knows to be wrong, and suffer the consequence whatever it may be. This is the key to the use of soul-force.

Reader : You would then disregard laws—this is rank disloyalty. We have always been considered a law-abiding nation. You seem to be going even beyond the extremists. They say that we must obey the laws that have been passed, but that if the laws be bad, we must drive out the law-givers even by force.

Editor : Whether I go beyond them or whether I do not is a matter of no consequence to either of us. We simply want to find out what is right and to act accordingly. The real meaning of the statement that we are a law-abiding nation is that we are passive resisters. When we do not like certain laws, we do not break the heads of law-givers but we suffer and do not submit to the laws. That we should obey laws whether good

1. The original has: "Satyagraha is referred to in English as passive resistance. The term denotes the method of . . . ."

or bad is a new-fangled notion. There was no such thing in former days. The people disregarded those laws they did not like and suffered the penalties for their breach. It is contrary to our manhood if we obey laws repugnant to our conscience. Such teaching is opposed to religion and means slavery. If the Government were to ask us to go about without any clothing,[1] should we do so? If I were a passive resister, I would say to them that I would have nothing to do with their law.[2] But we have so forgotten ourselves and become so compliant that we do not mind any degrading law.[3]

A man who has realized his manhood, who fears only God, will fear no one else. Man-made laws are not necessarily binding on him. Even the Government does not expect any such thing from us. They do not say: "You must do such and such a thing," but they say: "If you do not do it, we will punish you." We are sunk so low that we fancy that it is our duty and our religion to do what the law lays down. If man will only realize that it is unmanly to obey laws that are unjust, no man's tyranny will enslave him. This is the key to self-rule or home rule.

It is a superstition and ungodly thing to believe that an act of a majority binds a minority. Many examples can be given in which acts of majorities will be found to have been wrong and those of minorities to have been right. All reforms owe their origin to the initiation of minorities in opposition to majorities. If among a band of robbers a knowledge of robbing is obligatory, is a pious man to accept the obligation? So long as the superstition that men should obey unjust laws exists, so long will their slavery exist. And a passive resister alone can remove such a superstition.

To use brute-force, to use gunpowder, is contrary to passive resistance, for it means that we want our opponent to

1. The original has: "to strip ourselves naked and dance. . . ."
2. The original has: " . . . that I would do nothing of the kind, that I had no use for their law".
3. Literally, "But we lack the spirit of satyagraha to such an extent that when ordered by the Government, we do more degrading things than dance naked before it."

do by force that which we desire but he does not. And if such a use of force is justifiable, surely he is entitled to do likewise by us. And so we should never come to an agreement. We may simply fancy, like the blind horse[1] moving in a circle round a mill, that we are making progress. Those who believe that they are not bound to obey laws which are repugnant to their conscience have only the remedy of passive resistance open to them. Any other must lead to disaster.

Reader : From what you say I deduce that passive resistance is a splendid weapon of the weak, but that when they are strong they may take up arms.

Editor : This is gross ignorance. Passive resistance, that is, soul-force, is matchless. It is superior to the force of arms. How, then, can it be considered only a weapon of the weak? Physical-force men are strangers to the courage that is requisite in a passive resister. Do you believe that a coward can ever disobey a law that he dislikes? Extremists are considered to be advocates of brute force. Why do they, then, talk about obeying laws? I do not blame them. They can say nothing else. When they succeed in driving out the English and they themselves become governors, they will want you and me to obey their laws. And that is a fitting thing for their constitution. But a passive resister will say he will not obey a law that is against his conscience, even though he may be blown to pieces at the mouth of a cannon.

What do you think? Wherein is courage required—in blowing others to pieces from behind a cannon, or with a smiling face to approach a cannon and be blown to pieces? Who is the true warrior—he who keeps death always as a bosom-friend, or he who controls the death of others? Believe me that a man devoid of courage and manhood can never be a passive resister.

This, however, I will admit : that even a man weak in body is capable of offering this resistance. One man can offer it just as well as millions. Both men and women can indulge in it.[2] It

---

1. The original has: "bullock".
2. The original has: "A woman can offer it as well as a man."

does not require the training of an army; it needs no Jiu-Jitsu. Control over the mind is alone necessary, and when that is attained, man is free like the king of the forest and his very glance withers the enemy.

Passive resistance is an all-sided sword, it can be used anyhow; it blesses him who uses it and him against whom it is used. Without drawing a drop of blood it produces far-reaching results. It never rusts and cannot be stolen. Competition between passive resisters does not exhaust. The sword of passive resistance does not require a scabbard. It is strange indeed that you should consider such a weapon to be a weapon merely of the weak.

Reader : You have said that passive resistance is a speciality of India. Have cannons never been used in India?

Editor : Evidently, in your opinion, India means its few princes. To me it means its teeming millions on whom depends the existence of its princes and our own.

Kings will always use their kingly weapons. To use force is bred in them. They want to command, but those who have to obey commands do not want guns: and these are in a majority throughout the world. They have to learn either body-force or soul-force. Where they learn the former, both the rulers and the ruled become like so many madmen; but where they learn soul-force, the commands of the rulers do not go beyond the point of their swords, for true men disregard unjust commands. Peasants have never been subdued by the sword, and never will be. They do not know the use of the sword, and they are not frightened by the use of it by others. That nation is great which rests its head upon death as its pillow. Those who defy death are free from all fear.[1] For those who are labouring under the delusive charms of brute-force, this picture is not overdrawn. The fact is that, in India, the nation at large has generally used passive resistance in all departments of life. We cease to cooperate with our rulers when they displease us. This is passive resistance.

1. The original adds: "True, I am exaggerating somewhat."

I remember an instance when, in a small principality, the villagers were offended by some command issued by the prince. The former immediately began vacating the village. The prince became nervous, apologized to his subjects and withdrew his command. Many such instances can be found in India. Real Home Rule is possible only where passive resistance is the guiding force of the people. Any other rule is foreign rule.

Reader : Then you will say that it is not at all necessary for us to train the body?

Editor : I will certainly not say any such thing. It is difficult to become a passive resister unless the body is trained. As a rule, the mind, residing in a body that has become weakened by pampering, is also weak, and where there is no strength of mind there can be no strength of soul. We shall have to improve our physique by getting rid of infant marriages and luxurious living. If I were to ask a man with a shattered body to face a cannon's mouth, I should make a laughing-stock of myself.

Reader : From what you say, then, it would appear that it is not a small thing to become a passive resister, and, if that is so, I should like you to explain how a man may become one.

Editor : To become a passive resister is easy enough but it is also equally difficult. I have known a lad of fourteen years become a passive resister; I have known also sick people do likewise; and I have also known physically strong and otherwise happy people unable to take up passive resistance. After a great deal of experience it seems to me that those who want to become passive resisters for the service of the country have to observe perfect chastity, adopt poverty, follow truth, and cultivate fearlessness.

Chastity is one of the greatest disciplines without which the mind cannot attain requisite firmness. A man who is unchaste loses stamina, becomes emasculated and cowardly. He whose mind is given over to animal passions is not capable of any great effort. This can be proved by innumerable instances. What, then, is a married person to do is the question that arises naturally; and yet it need not. When a husband and wife gratify the passions, it is no less an animal indulgence on that account. Such an indulgence, except for perpetuating the race, is strictly prohibited. But a passive resister has to avoid even that very limited indulgence because he can have no desire for progeny. A married man, therefore, can observe perfect chastity. This subject is not capable of being treated at greater length. Several questions arise: How is one to carry one's wife with one, what are her rights, and other similar questions. Yet those who wish to take part in a great work are bound to solve these puzzles.

Just as there is necessity for chastity, so is there for poverty. Pecuniary ambition and passive resistance cannot well go together. Those who have money are not expected to throw it away, but they are expected to be indifferent about it. They must be prepared to lose every penny rather than give up passive resistance.

Passive resistance has been described in the course of our discussion as truth-force. Truth, therefore, has necessarily to be followed and that at any cost[1]. In this connection, academic questions such as whether a man may not lie in order to save a life, etc., arise, but these questions occur only to those who wish to justify lying. Those who want to follow truth every time are not placed in such a quandary; and if they are, they are still saved from a false position.

Passive resistance cannot proceed a step without fearlessness. Those alone can follow the path of passive resistance who are free from fear, whether as to their possessions, false honour, their relatives, the government, bodily injuries or death.

These observances are not to be abandoned in the belief that they are difficult. Nature has implanted in the human breast ability to cope with any difficulty or suffering that may come to man unprovoked. These qualities are worth having, even for those who do not wish to serve the country. Let there

1. Instead of these two sentences, the original has: "How can anyone command the power of truth unless he dedicates himself to truth? Truth, therefore, is absolutely necessary. It cannot be abandoned, whatever the cost. Truth has nothing to hide. There is no question, therefore, of a satyagrahi maintaining a secret army."

be no mistake, as those who want to train themselves in the use of arms are also obliged to have these qualities more or less. Everybody does not become a warrior for the wish. A would-be warrior will have to observe chastity and to be satisfied with poverty as his lot. A warrior without fearlessness cannot be conceived of. It may be thought that he would not need to be exactly truthful, but that quality follows real fearlessness. When a man abandons truth, he does so owing to fear in some shape or form. The above four attributes, then, need not frighten anyone. It may be as well here to note that a physical-force man has to have many other useless qualities which a passive resister never needs. And you will find that whatever extra effort a swordsman needs is due to lack of fearlessness. If he is an embodiment of the latter, the sword will drop from his hand that very moment. He does not need its support. One who is free from hatred requires no sword. A man with a stick suddenly came face to face with a lion and instinctively raised his weapon in self-defence. The man saw that he had only prated about fearlessness when there was none in him. That moment he dropped the stick and found himself free from all fear.

18

Education

Reader : In the whole of our discussion, you have not demonstrated the necessity for education; we always complain of its absence among us. We notice a movement for compulsory education in our country. The Maharaja Gaekwar has introduced it in his territories. Every eye is directed towards them. We bless the Maharaja for it. Is all this effort then of no use?

Editor : If we consider our civilization to be the highest, I have regretfully to say that much of the effort you have described is of no use. The motive of the Maharaja and other great leaders who have been working in this direction is perfectly pure. They, therefore, undoubtedly deserve great praise. But we cannot conceal from ourselves the result that is likely to flow from their effort.

What is the meaning of education? It simply means a knowledge of letters. It is merely an instrument, and an instrument may be well used or abused. The same instrument that may be used to cure a patient may be used to take his life, and so may be a knowledge of letters. We daily observe that many men abuse it and very few make good use of it; and if this is a correct statement, we have proved that more harm has been done by it than good.

The ordinary meaning of education is a knowledge of letters. To teach boys reading, writing and arithmetic is called primary education. A peasant earns his bread honestly. He has ordinary knowledge of the world. He knows fairly well how he should behave towards his parents, his wife, his children and his fellow-villagers. He understands and observes the rules of morality. But he cannot write his own name. What do you propose to do by giving him a knowledge of letters? Will you add an inch to his happiness? Do you wish to make him discontented with his cottage or his lot? And even if you want to do that, he will not need such an education. Carried away by the flood of western thought we came to the conclusion, without weighing pros and cons, that we should give this kind of education to the people.

Now let us take higher education. I have learned Geography, Astronomy, Algebra, Geometry, etc.[1] What of that? In what way have I benefited myself or those around me? Why have I learned these things ? Professor Huxley has thus defined education:

> That man I think has had a liberal education who has been so trained in youth that his body is the ready servant of his will and does with ease and pleasure all the work that as a mechanism it is capable of; whose intellect is a clear, cold, logic[al] engine with all its parts of equal strength and in smooth working order . . .[2] whose mind is stored with a knowledge of the fundamental truths of nature . . . whose passions are trained to come to heel by a vigorous will, the servant of a tender conscience . . . who has learnt to hate all vileness and to respect others as himself. Such a one and no other, I conceive, has had a liberal education, for he is in harmony with nature. He will make the best of her and she of him.

If this is true education, I must emphatically say that the sciences I have enumerated above I have never been able to use for controlling my senses. Therefore, whether you take elementary education or higher education, it is not required for the main thing. It does not make men of us. It does not enable us to do our duty.

Reader : If that is so, I shall have to ask you another question : What enables you to tell all these things to me? If

1. The original adds: "and dabbled in Geology".
2. The words for "with all . . . order" are not found in the original.

you had not received higher education, how would you have been able to explain to me the things that you have?

Editor : You have spoken well.[1] But my answer is simple: I do not for one moment believe that my life would have been wasted, had I not received higher or lower education. Nor do I consider that I necessarily serve because I speak. But I do desire to serve and in endeavouring to fulfil that desire, I make use of the education I have received. And, if I am making good use of it, even then it is not for the millions, but I can use it only for such as you, and this supports my contention. Both you and I have come under the bane of what is mainly false education. I claim to have become free from its ill effect, and I am trying to give you the benefit of my experience and in doing so, I am demonstrating the rottenness of this education.

Moreover,[2] I have not run down a knowledge of letters in all circumstances. All I have now shown is that we must not make of it a fetish. It is not our *Kamadhuk*[3]. In its place it can be of use and it has its place when we have brought our senses under subjection and put our ethics on a firm foundation. And then, if we feel inclined to receive that education, we may make good use of it. As an ornament it is likely to sit well on us. It now follows that it is not necessary to make this education compulsory. Our ancient school system is enough. Character building has the first place in it and that is primary education. A building erected on that foundation will last.

Reader : Do I then understand that you do not consider English education necessary for obtaining Home Rule?

Editor : My answer is yes and no. To give millions a knowledge of English is to enslave them. The foundation that Macaulay laid of education has enslaved us. I do not suggest that he had any such intention, but that has been the result. Is it not a sad commentary that we should have to speak of Home Rule in a foreign tongue?

And it is worthy of note that the systems which the Europeans have discarded systems in vogue among us. Their

---

1. Literally, "This is a brave attack indeed."
2. The original adds: "Your attack is ill-conceived, for".
3. Mythical cow, yielding whatever is wished for.

learned men continually make changes. We ignorantly adhere to their cast-off systems. They are trying each division to improve its own status. Wales is a small portion of England.[1] Great efforts are being made to revive a knowledge of Welsh among Welshmen. The English Chancellor, Mr.Lloyd George, is taking a leading part in the movement to make Welsh children speak Welsh. And what is our condition? We write to each in faulty English, and from this even our M.As. are not free; our best thoughts are expressed in English; the proceedings of our Congress are conducted in English; our best newspapers are printed in English. If this state of things continues for a long time, posterity will—it is my firm opinion—condemn and curse us.

It is worth noting that, by receiving English education, we have enslaved the nation. Hypocrisy, tyranny, etc., have increased; English-knowing Indians have not hesitated to cheat and strike terror into the people. Now, if we are doing anything for the people at all, we are paying only a portion of the debt due to them.

Is it not a painful thing that, if I want to go to a court of justice, I must employ the English language as a medium, that when I become a barrister, I may not speak my mother-tongue and that someone else should have to translate to me from my own language? Is not this absolutely absurd? Is it not a sign of slavery? Am I to blame the English for it or myself? It is we, the English-knowing Indians, that have enslaved India. The curse of the nation will rest not upon the English but upon us.

I have told you that my answer to your last question is both yes and no. I have explained to you why it is yes. I shall now explain why it is no.

We are so much beset by the disease of civilization, that we cannot altogether do without English education. Those who have already received it may make good use of it wherever necessary. In our dealings with the English people, in our dealings with our own people, when we can only correspond with them through that language, and for the purpose of

1. The original adds: "Its language is no language at all".

knowing how disgusted they (the English) have themselves become with their civilization, we may use or learn English, as the case may be. Those who have studied English will have to teach morality to their progeny through their mother-tongue and to teach them another Indian language; but when they have grown up, they may learn English, the ultimate aim being that we should not need it. The object of making money thereby should be eschewed. Even in learning English to such a limited extent we shall have to consider what we should learn through it and what we should not. It will be necessary to know what sciences we should learn. A little thought should show you that immediately we cease to care for English degrees, the rulers will prick up their ears.

Reader : Then what education shall we give ?

Editor : This has been somewhat considered above, but we will consider it a little more. I think that we have to improve all our languages. What subjects we should learn through them need not be elaborated here. Those English books which are valuable, we should translate into the various Indian languages. We should abandon the pretension of learning many sciences. Religious, that is ethical, education will occupy the first place. Every cultured Indian will know in addition to his own provincial language, if a Hindu, Sanskrit; if a Mahomedan, Arabic; if a Parsee, Persian; and all, Hindi. Some Hindus should know Arabic and Persian; some Mahomedans and Parsees, Sanskrit. Several Northerners and Westerners should learn Tamil. A universal language for India should be Hindi, with the option of writing it in Persian or Nagari characters. In order that the Hindus and the Mahomedans may have closer relations, it is necessary to know both the characters. And, if we can do this, we can drive the English language out of the field in a short time. All this is necessary for us, slaves. Through our slavery the nation has been enslaved, and it will be free with our freedom.

Reader : The question of religious education is very difficult.

Editor : Yet we cannot do without it. India will never be godless. Rank atheism cannot flourish in this land. The task is indeed difficult. My head begins to turn as I think of religious education. Our religious teachers are hypocritical and selfish; they will have to be approached. The Mullas[1] the Dasturs[2] and the Brahmins hold the key in their hands, but if they will not have the good sense, the energy that we have derived from English education will have to be devoted to religious education. This is not very difficult. Only the fringe of the ocean has been polluted and it is those who are within the fringe who alone need cleansing. We who come under this category can even cleanse ourselves because my remarks do not apply to the millions. In order to restore India to its pristine condition, we have to return to it. In our own civilization there will naturally be progress, retrogression, reforms, and reactions; but one effort is required, and that is to drive out Western civilization. All else will follow.

1. Muslim divines.
2. Parsee priests.

19

Machinery

Reader : When you speak of driving out Western civilization, I suppose you will also say that we want no machinery.

Editor : By raising this question you have opened the wound I have received.[1] When I read Mr. Dutt's *Economic History of India,* I wept; and as I think of it again my heart sickens. It is machinery that has impoverished India. It is difficult to measure the harm that Manchester has done to us. It is due to Manchester that Indian handicraft has all but disappeared.

But I make a mistake. How can Manchester be blamed? We wore Manchester cloth and this is why Manchester wove it. I was delighted when I read about the bravery of Bengal.[2] There were no cloth-mills in that Presidency. They were, therefore, able to restore the original hand-weaving occupation. It is true Bengal encourages the mill-industry of Bombay. If Bengal had proclaimed a boycott of *all* machine-made goods, it would have been much better.

Machinery has begun to desolate Europe. Ruination is now knocking at the English[3] gates. Machinery is the chief symbol of modern civilization; it represents a great sin.[4]

The workers in the mills of Bombay have become slaves. The condition of the women working in the mills is shocking. When there were no mills, these women were not starving. If

1. The original has: "You have re-opened my wound."
2. The reference, obviously, is to the Swadeshi Movement.
3. The original has "Indian".
4. The original has: "I am convinced that it . . ."

the machinery craze grows in our country, it will become an unhappy land. It may be considered a heresy, but I am bound to say that it were better for us to send money to Manchester and to use flimsy Manchester cloth than to multiply mills in India. By using Manchester cloth we only waste our money; but by reproducing Manchester in India, we shall keep our money at the price of our blood, because our very moral being will be sapped, and I call in support of my statement the very mill-hands as witnesses. And those who have amassed wealth out of factories are not likely to be better than other rich men. It would be folly to assume that an Indian Rockefeller would be better than the American Rockefeller. Impoverished India can become free, but it will be hard for any India made rich through immorality to regain its freedom. I fear we shall have to admit that moneyed men support British rule; their interest is bound up with its stability. Money renders a man helpless. The other thing which is equally harmful is sexual vice. Both are poison. A snakebite is a lesser poison than these two, because the former merely destroys the body but the latter destroys body, mind and soul. We need not, therefore, be pleased with the prospect of the growth of the mill-industry.

Reader : Are the mills, then, to be closed down?

Editor : That is difficult. It is no easy task to do away with a thing that is established. We, therefore, say that the non-beginning of a thing is supreme wisdom. We cannot condemn millowners; we can but pity them. It would be too much to expect them to give up their mills, but we may implore them not to increase them. If they would be good they would gradually contract their business. They can establish in thousands of households the ancient and sacred handlooms and they can buy out the cloth that may be thus woven. Whether the mill owners do this or not, people can cease to use machine-made goods.

Reader : You have so far spoken about machine-made cloth, but there are innumerable machine-made things. We have either to import them or to introduce machinery into our country.

Editor : Indeed, our goods even are made in Germany. What need, then, to speak of matches, pins and glassware ? My answer can be only one. What did India do before these articles were introduced? Precisely the same should be done today. As long as we cannot make pins without machinery, so long will we do without them. The tinsel splendour of glassware we will have nothing to do with, and we will make wicks, as of old, with home-grown cotton and use hand-made earthen saucers or lamps. So doing, we shall save our eyes and money and support *swadeshi* and so shall we attain Home Rule.

It is not to be conceived that all men will do all these things at one time or that some men will give up all machine-made things at once. But, if the thought is sound, we shall always find out what we can give up and gradually cease to use it. What a few may do, others will copy; and the movement will grow like the coconut of the mathematical problem. What the leaders do, the populace will gladly do in turn. The matter is neither complicated nor difficult. You and I need not wait until we can carry others with us. Those will be the losers who will not do it, and those who will not do it, although they appreciate the truth, will deserve to be called cowards[1].

Reader : What, then, of the tram-cars and electricity?

Editor : This question is now too late. It signifies nothing. If we are to do without the railways we shall have to do without the tramcars. Machinery is like a snake-hole which may contain from one to a hundred snakes. Where there is machinery there are large cities; and where there are large cities, there are tram-cars and railways; and there only does one see electric light. English villages do not boast of any of these things. Honest physicians will tell you that where means of artificial locomotion have increased, the health of the people has suffered. I remember that when in a European town there was a scarcity of money, the receipts of the tramway company, of the lawyers and of the doctors went down and people were less unhealthy. I cannot recall a single good point in connection with machinery. Books can be written to demonstrate its evils.

---

1. Literally, "hypocrites".

Reader : Is it a good point or a bad one that all you are saying will be printed through machinery?

Editor : This is one of those instances which demonstrate that sometimes poison is used to kill poison. This, then, will not be a good point regarding machinery. As it expires, the machinery, as it were, says to us: "Beware and avoid me. You will derive no benefits from me and the benefit that may accrue from printing will avail only those who are infected with the machinery-craze."

Do not, therefore, forget the main thing. It is necessary to realize that machinery is bad. We shall then be able gradually to do away with it. Nature has not provided any way whereby we may reach a desired goal all of a sudden. If, instead of welcoming machinery as a boon, we should look upon it as an evil, it would ultimately go.

20

Conclusion

Reader : From your views I gather that you would form a third party. You are neither an extremist nor a moderate.

Editor : That is a mistake. I do not think of a third party at all. We do not all think alike. We cannot say that all the moderates hold identical views. And how can those who want only to serve have a party ? I would serve both the moderates and the extremists. Where I differ from them, I would respectfully place my position before them and continue my service.

Reader : What, then, would you say to both the parties?

Editor : I would say to the extremists: "I know that you want Home Rule for India; it is not to be had for your asking. Everyone will have to take it for himself. What others get for me is not Home Rule but foreign rule; therefore, it would not be proper for you to say that you have obtained Home Rule if you have merely expelled the English. I have already described the true nature of Home Rule. This you would never obtain by force of arms. Brute force is not natural to Indian soil. You will have, therefore, to rely wholly on soul-force. You must not consider that violence is necessary at any stage for reaching our goal."

I would say to the moderates: "Mere petitioning is derogatory; we thereby confess inferiority. To say that British rule is indispensable is almost a denial of the Godhead. We cannot say that anybody or anything is indispensable except God. Moreover, commonsense should tell us that to state that, for the time being, the presence of the English in India is a necessity, is to make them conceited.

"If the English vacated India, bag and baggage, it must not be supposed that she would be widowed. It is possible that those who are forced to observe peace under their pressure would fight after their withdrawal. There can be no advantage in suppressing an eruption; it must have its vent. If, therefore, before we can remain at peace, we must fight amongst ourselves, it is better that we do so. There is no occasion for a third party to protect the weak. It is this socalled protection which has unnerved us. Such protection can only make the weak weaker. Unless we realize this, we cannot have Home Rule. I would paraphrase the thought of an English divine and say that anarchy under Home Rule were better than orderly foreign rule. Only, the meaning that the learned divine attached to Home Rule is different from Indian Home Rule according to my conception. We have to learn, and to teach others, that we do not want the tyranny of either English rule or Indian rule."

If this idea were carried out, both the extremists and the moderates could[1] join hands. There is no occasion to fear or distrust one another.

Reader : What, then, would you say to the English?

Editor : To them I would respectfully say: "I admit you are my rulers. It is not necessary to debate the question whether you hold India by the sword or by my consent. I have no objection to your remaining in my country, but although you are the rulers, you will have to remain as servants of the people. It is not we who have to do as you wish, but it is you who have to do as we wish. You may keep the riches that you have drained away from this land, but you may not drain riches henceforth. Your function will be, if you so wish, to police India; you must abandon the idea of deriving any commercial benefit from us. We hold the civilization that you support to be the reverse of civilization. We consider our civilization to be far superior to yours. If you realize this truth, it will be to your advantage and, if you do not, according to your own proverb, you should only live in our country in the same manner as we

1. The original has: "will join hands, they can, they must".

do.[1] You must not do anything that is contrary to our religions. It is your duty as rulers that for the sake of the Hindus you should eschew beef, and for the sake of Mahomedans you should avoid bacon and ham. We have hitherto said nothing because we have been cowed down, but you need not consider that you have not hurt our feelings by your conduct. We are not expressing our sentiments either through base selfishness or fear, but because it is our duty now to speak out boldly. We consider your schools and law courts to be useless. We want our own ancient schools and courts to be restored. The common language of India is not English but Hindi. You should, therefore, learn it. We can hold communication with you only in our national language. "We cannot tolerate the idea of your spending money on railways and the military. We see no occasion for either. You may fear Russia; we do not. When she comes we shall look after her. If you are with us, we may then receive her jointly. We do not need any European cloth. We shall manage with articles produced and manufactured at home. You may not keep one eye on Manchester and the other on India. We can work together only if our interests are identical.

"This has not been said to you in arrogance. You have great military resources. Your naval power is matchless. If we wanted to fight with you on your own ground, we should be unable to do so, but if the above submissions be not acceptable to you, we cease to play the part of the ruled. You may, if you like, cut us to pieces. You may shatter us at the cannon's mouth. If you act contrary to our will, we shall not help you; and without our help, we know that you cannot move one step forward.

"It is likely that you will laugh at all this in the intoxication of your power. We may not be able to disillusion you at once; but if there be any manliness in us, you will see shortly that your intoxication is suicidal and that your laugh at our expense is an aberration of intellect. We believe that at heart you belong to a religious nation. We are living in a land which is the source

1. A reference to: "When in Rome, do as the Romans do."

of religions. How we came together need not be considered, but we can make mutual good use of our relations.

"You, English, who have come to India are not good specimens of the English nation, nor can we, almost half-Anglicized Indians, be considered good specimens of the real Indian nation. If the English nation were to know all you have done, it would oppose many of your actions. The mass of the Indians have had few dealings with you. If you will abandon your so-called civilization and search into your own scriptures, you will find that our demands are just. Only on condition of our demands being fully satisfied may you remain in India; and if you remain under those conditions, we shall learn several things from you and you will learn many from us. So doing we shall benefit each other and the world. But that will happen only when the root of our relationship is sunk in a religious soil."

Reader : What will you say to the nation ?

Editor : Who is the nation ?

Reader : For our purposes it is the nation that you and I have been thinking of, that is, those of us who are affected by European civilization, and who are eager to have Home Rule.

Editor : To these I would say: "It is only those Indians who are imbued with real love who will be able to speak to the English in the above strain without being frightened, and only those can be said to be so imbued who conscientiously believe that Indian civilization is the best and that the European is a nine days' wonder. Such ephemeral civilizations have often come and gone and will continue to do so. Those only can be considered to be so imbued who, having experienced the force of the soul within themselves, will not cower before brute force, and will not, on any account, desire to use brute force. Those only can be considered to have been so imbued who are intensely dissatisfied with the present pitiable condition, having already drunk the cup of poison.

"If there be only one such Indian, he will speak as above to the English and the English will have to listen to him.

"These are not demands, but they show our mental state. We shall get nothing by asking; we shall have to take what we want, and we need the requisite strength for the effort and that strength will be available to him only who will act thus:

1. He will only on rare occasions make use of the English language.
2. If a lawyer, he will give up his profession, and take up a handloom.
3. If a lawyer, he will devote his knowledge to enlightening both his people and the English.
4. If a lawyer, he will not meddle with the quarrels between parties but will give up the courts, and from his experience induce the people to do likewise.
5. If a lawyer, he will refuse to be a judge, as he will give up his profession.
6. If a doctor, he will give up medicine, and understand that rather than mending bodies, he should mend souls.
7. If a doctor, he will understand that no matter to what religion he belongs, it is better that bodies remain diseased rather than that they are cured through the instrumentality of the diabolical vivisection that is practised in European schools of medicine.
8. Although a doctor, he will take up a handloom, and if any patients come to him, will tell them the cause of their diseases, and will advise them to remove the cause rather than pamper them by giving useless drugs; he will understand that if by not taking drugs, perchance the patient dies, the world will not come to grief and that he will have been really merciful to him.
9. Although a wealthy man, yet regardless of his wealth, he will speak out his mind and fear no one.
10. If a wealthy man, he will devote his money to establishing handlooms, and encourage others to use hand-made goods by wearing them himself.
11. Like every other Indian, he will know that this is a time for repentance, expiation and mourning.
12. Like every other Indian, he will know that to blame the English is useless, that they came because of us, and remain also for the same reason, and that they will either go or change their nature only when we reform ourselves.

13. Like others, he will understand that at a time of mourning, there can be no indulgence, and that, whilst we are in a fallen state, to be in gaol or in banishment is much the best.
14. Like others, he will know that it is superstition to imagine it necessary that we should guard against being imprisoned in order that we may deal with the people.
15. Like others, he will know that action is much better than speech; that it is our duty to say exactly what we think and face the consequences and that it will be only then that we shall be able to impress anybody with our speech.
16. Like others, he will understand that we shall become free only through suffering.
17. Like others, he will understand that deportation for life to the Andamans is not enough expiation for the sin of encouraging European civilization.
18. Like others, he will know that no nation has risen without suffering; that, even in physical warfare, the true test is suffering and not the killing of others, much more so in the warfare of passive resistance.
19. Like others, he will know that it is an idle excuse to say that we shall do a thing when the others also do it; that we should do what we know to be right, and that others will do it when they see the way; that when I fancy a particular delicacy, I do not wait till others taste it; that to make a national effort and to suffer are in the nature of delicacies; and that to suffer under pressure is no suffering."

Reader : This is a large order. When will all carry it out ?

Editor : You make a mistake, you and I have nothing to do with the others. Let each do his duty.[1] If I do my duty, that is, serve myself, I shall be able to serve others.[2]

1. The original has: " 'You mind your own business and leave me to mine' is taken to be an expression of a selfish attitude, but in fact it tends to public good."
2. The original adds: "I shall have done enough for success in the given task if I do my duty well."

Before I leave you, I will take the liberty of repeating :

1. Real home-rule is self-rule or self-control.
2. The way to it is passive resistance : that is soul-force or love-force.
3. In order to exert this force, *swadeshi* in every sense is necessary.
4. What we want to do should be done, not because we object to the English or because we want to retaliate but because it is our duty to do so. Thus, supposing that the English remove the salt-tax, restore our money, give the highest posts to Indians, withdraw the English troops, we shall certainly not use their machine-made goods, nor use the English language, nor many of their industries. It is worth noting that these things are, in their nature, harmful; hence we do not want them. I bear no enmity towards the English but I do towards their civilization.

In my opinion, we have used the term *"swaraj"* without understanding its real significance. I have endeavoured to explain it as I understand it, and my conscience testifies that my life henceforth is dedicated to its attainment.

Appendices

APPENDIX I

Some Authorities

The following books are recommended for perusal to follow up the study of the foregoing :

The Kingdom of God is within You (Tolstoy)

What is Art? (Tolstoy)

The Slavery of our Times (Tolstoy)

The First Step (Tolstoy)

How shall We Escape? (Tolstoy)

Letter to a Hindoo (Tolstoy)

The White Slaves of England (Sherard)

Civilization, its Cause and Cure (Carpenter)

The Fallacy of Speed (Taylor)

A New Crusade (Blount)

On the Duty of Civil Disobedience (Thoreau)

Life without Principle (Thoreau)

Unto this Last (Ruskin)

A Joy for Ever (Ruskin)

Duties of Man (Mazzini)

Defence and Death of Socrates (from Plato)

Paradoxes of Civilization (Max Nordau)

Poverty and Un-British Rule in India (Naoroji)

Economic History of India (Dutt)

Village Communities (Maine)

APPENDIX II

Testimonies by Eminent Men

The following extracts from Mr. Alfred Webb's valuable collection show that the ancient Indian civilization has little to learn from the modern :

J. SEYMOUR KEAY, M. P.
BANKER in INDIA and INDIA AGENT
(Writing in 1883)

It cannot be too well understood that our position in India has never been in any degree that of civilians bringing civilization to savage races. When we landed in India we found there a hoary civilization, which, during the progress of thousands of years, had fitted into the character and adjusted itself to the wants of highly intellectual races. The civilization was not perfunctory, but universal and all-pervading—furnishing the country not only with political systems, but with social and domestic institutions of the most ramified description. The beneficent nature of these institutions as a whole may be judged from their effects on the character of the Hindu race. Perhaps there are no other people in the world who show so much in their character the advantageous effects of their own civilization. They are shrewd in business, acute in reasoning, thrifty, religious, sober, charitable, obedient to parents, reverential to old age, amiable, law abiding, compassionate towards the helpless and patient under suffering.

VICTOR COUSIN (1792-1867)
FOUNDER of SYSTEMATIC ECLECTICISM in PHILOSOPHY

On the other hand when we read with attention the poetical and philosophical movements of the East, above all, those of India, which are beginning to spread in Europe, we discover there so many truths, and truths, so profound, and which make such a contrast with the meanness of the results at which the European genius has sometimes stopped, that we are constrained to bend the knee before that of the East, and do see in this cradle of the human race the native land of the highest philosophy.

FRIEDRICH MAX MULLER

If I were to ask myself from what literature we here in Europe, we who have been nurtured almost exclusively on the thoughts of Greeks and Romans, and of one Semitic race, the Jewish, may draw that corrective which is most wanted in order to make our inner life more perfect, more comprehensive, more universal, in fact more truly human, a life, not for this life only, but a transfigured and eternal life—again I should point to India.

FREDERICK VON SCHLEGEL

It cannot be denied that the early Indians possessed a knowledge of the true God; all their writings are replete with sentiments and expressions, noble, clear, and severely grand, as deeply conceived and reverently expressed as in any human language in which men have spoken of their God. . . . Among nations possessing indigenous philosophy and metaphysics together with an innate relish for these pursuits, such as at present characterizes Germany, and, in olden times was the proud distinction of Greece, Hindustan holds the first rank in point of time.

1. The original edition printed by the International Printing Press in 1910 had after Max Müller's testimony the following :

Michael G. Mulhall, F. R. S. S.

Statistics

PRISON POPULATION PER 100,000 OF INHABITANTS

Several European States....	100 to 230
England and Wales....	90
India	38

Dictionary of Statistics, M. G. Mulhall, F. R. S. S., Routledge & Sons, 1899.

ABBE J. A. DUBOIS

MISSIONARY in MYSORE

Extracts from a letter dated December 15, 1820, Seringapatam: December, 1820, Seringapatam:

The authority of married women within their houses is chiefly exerted in preserving good order and peace among the persons who compose their families; and a great many among them discharge this important duty with a prudence and a discretion which have scarcely a parallel in Europe. I have known families composed of between thirty and forty persons, or more, consisting of grown up sons and daughters, all married and all having children, living together under the superintendence of an old matron—their mother or mother-in-law. The latter, by good management, and by accommodating herself to the temper of the daughters-in-law, by using, according to circumstances, firmness or forbearance, succeeded in preserving peace and harmony during many years amongst so many females, who had all jarring tempers. I ask you whether it would be possible to attain the same end, in the same circumstances, in our countries, where it is scarcely possible to make two women living under the same roof to agree together.

In fact, there is perhaps no kind of honest employment in a civilized country in which the Hindu females have not a due share. Besides the management of the household, and the care of the family which (as already noticed is under their control, the wives and daughters of husbandmen attend and assist their husbands and fathers in the labours of agriculture. Those of tradesmen assist theirs in carrying on their trade. Merchants are attended and assisted by theirs in their shops. Many females are shopkeepers on their own account; and *without a knowledge of the alphabet* or of the decimal scale, they keep by other means their accounts in excellent order, and are considered as still shrewder than the males themselves in their commercial dealings.

J. YOUNG
SECRETARY, SAVON MECHANICS INSTITUTES within RECENT YEARS

Those races (the Indian viewed from a moral aspect) are perhaps the most remarkable people in the world. They breathe in an atmosphere of moral purity, which cannot but excite admiration, and this is especially the case with the poorer classes, who, notwithstanding the privations of their humble lot, appear to be happy and contented. True children of nature, they live on from day to day, taking no thought for the morrow and thankful for the simple fare which Providence has provided for them. It is curious to witness the spectacle of coolies of both sexes returning home at nightfall after a hard day's work often lasting from sunrise to sunset. In spite of fatigue from the effects of the unremitting toil, they are, for the most part, gay and animated, conversing cheerfully together and occasionally breaking into snatches of light-hearted song. Yet what awaits them on their return to the hovels which they call home? A dish of rice for food, and the floor for a bed. Domestic felicity appears to be the rule among the Natives, and this is the more strange when the customs of marriage are taken into account, parents arranging all such matters. Many Indian households afford examples of the married state in its highest degree of perfection. This may be due to the teachings of the *Shastras*, and to the strict injunctions which they inculcate with regard to marital obligation; but it is no exaggeration to say that husbands are generally devotedly attached to their wives, and in many instances the latter have the most exalted conception of their duties towards their husbands.

COLONEL THOMAS MUNRO
THIRTY-TWO YEARS' SERVICE in INDIA

If a good system of agriculture, unrivalled manufacturing skill, a capacity to produce whatever can contribute to convenience or luxury; schools established in every village for teaching reading, writing and arithmetic; the general practice of hospitality and charity among each other; and, above all, a treatment of the female sex, full of confidence, respect and delicacy, are among the signs which denote a civilized people, then the Hindus are not inferior to the nations of Europe; and if civilization is to become an article of trade between the two countries, I am convinced that this country [England] will gain by the import cargo.

SIR WILLIAM WEDDERBURN, BART

The Indian village has thus for centuries remained a bulwark against political disorder, and the home of the simple domestic and social virtues. No wonder, therefore, that philosophers and historians have always dwelt lovingly on this ancient institution which is the natural social unit and the best type of rural life: self-contained, industrious, peace-loving, conservative in the best sense of the word. . . . I think you will agree with me that there is much that is both picturesque and attractive in this glimpse of social and domestic life in an Indian village. It is a harmless and happy form of human existence. Moreover, it is not without good practical outcome.

Index